Christian Doctrine and the Grammar of Difference

Christian Doctrine and the Grammar of Difference

A Contribution to Feminist Systematic Theology

Janice McRandal

Fortress Press
Minneapolis

CHRISTIAN DOCTRINE AND THE GRAMMAR OF DIFFERENCE

A Contribution to Feminist Systematic Theology

Cover design: Alisha Lofgren

Library of Congress Cataloging-in-Publication Data

Print ISBN: 978-14514-8447-2

eBook ISBN: 978-1-4514-9424-2

The paper used in this publication meets the minimum requirements of American National Standard for Information Sciences — Permanence of Paper for Printed Library Materials, ANSI Z329.48-1984.

Manufactured in the U.S.A.

This book was produced using PressBooks.com, and PDF rendering was done by PrinceXML.

Contents

Part III. Trinity

Acknowledgements

This manuscript is the result of a PhD thesis completed at Charles Sturt University. I am grateful for all the support I received during the writing of this thesis. Charles Sturt University and the Public and Contextual Theology research centre provided significant resources over the course of writing. Steve Wright, Matthew Wilcoxen, Ian Packer, and Damian Palmer have each provided wonderful friendship and solidarity throughout the process. Joy McDougall, Stephen Burns, and Eugene Rogers, each provided substantial feedback and helped crystalize many of the ideas developed in this work. My supervisor and friend, Ben Myers, has shown profound grace and patience towards me; this has meant far more than my thanks can express. I offer a heartfelt thanks to my friends at WomeninTheology for their ongoing encouragement and camaraderie. A special acknowledgment is due my dear friend Rebecca Cundasamy, who has cared for me so well over the last year. Likewise for Peter Kline, who not only provided support in the preparation of this manuscript, but whose loving kindness has been nothing short of life-changing. And finally: to Jesse and Penelope, thank you.

Introduction: Feminist Theology, Difference, and Christian Discourse

It is hard to imagine a more optimistic beginning than the early movement of second-wave feminist theology.[1] Bolstered by the momentum of secular feminism[2] and by a boundless confidence in the critique of Christian orthodoxy, these pioneering scholars set about the task of liberating all women. It is easy to appreciate this initial enthusiasm. As Rosemary Radford Ruether notes, the fundamental impetus for change was at first simply to challenge the patriarchal notion that women are inferior.[3] The fight for equality ensured that feminist scholars across all disciplines would argue for

---

1. The feminist movement has been categorized by three distinctive "waves." The first wave—during the nineteenth and early twentieth century—focused on the pragmatic issues of women's education and the right to vote and was debated primarily in the United Kingdom and North America. The second wave came to prominence in the United States in the early nineteen sixties. Third-wave feminism is generally accepted as the period of feminism arising in the early nineteen eighties. The distinction between second- and third-wave feminisms is discussed in this book.

2. There is no doubt that Betty Friedan's *The Feminist Mystique* was the first major publication of second-wave feminist thought; however writers such as Gloria Steinem, Germaine Greer, and Kate Millett are just some of the highly successful feminists to catapult the "feminist question" into broader disciplinary inquiry; including Christian theology. See Betty Friedan, *The Feminist Mystique* (New York: W.W. Norton and Co., 1963).

3. Rosemary Radford Ruether, "The Emergence of Christian Feminist Theology," in *The Cambridge Companion to Feminist Theology*, ed. Susan Frank Parsons (Cambridge: Cambridge University Press, 2002), 3.

the status of women alongside men, especially in regard to the qualities favored by Enlightenment philosophers: rational thinking and moral judgement. This early feminism was thus aptly noted for an "enthusiasm for sameness."[4] Society was being charged with blindly, wilfully even, failing to see that women are in fact the same as men. However, to be rightly elevated to the lofty status of "sameness," women needed to convince the world that they had been—that they were indeed still being—oppressed. A central strategy in this regard was the concept of consciousness raising, together with appeals to women's experience.[5] There was a strong belief that if women could share their stories with the wider community then a consensus would emerge regarding the need for revolution. Certainly, such appeals had a positive effect with respect to women's opportunities, especially in North America. And yet the process also revealed something deeply problematic about early second-wave feminism, for the experiences being shared, the consciousness being raised, and the opportunities being granted were almost exclusively for the *same* kind of woman: white middle-class woman.

African Americans such as Alice Walker led stinging attacks on the privileging of white women's experience and the preposterous claim that a housewife from the suburbs could ever speak about the oppression of a North American black woman.[6] In response, womanist theologians sought to share the experience of women who were oppressed primarily because of race. The critique of categorizing experience grew with the inception of Mujerista theologies,[7] which challenged feminists to consider the experience of

4. Susan F. Parsons, "The Dilemma of Difference: A Feminist Theological Exploration," *Feminist Theology: The Journal of the Britain & Ireland School of Feminist Theology* 14, no. 5 (1997): 53.
5. Seen as a form of political activism, consciousness-raising groups were pioneered by the second-wave feminist alliance known as the "New York Radical Women."
6. See Alice Walker, *In Search of Our Mothers' Gardens: Womanist Prose* (New York: Harcourt Brace Jovanovich, 1983).

Latinas living in the United States. Questions of race and class became critical factors as feminist theology attempted to define its boundaries and cement a definite methodology. Further questions of colonialism saw the emergence of influential feminist theologians such as Kwok Pui-Lan and Mercy Amba Oduyoye, writing from Asian and African perspectives, respectively.[8] In each new representation, the critique of second-wave white feminism became more forceful. It was clear that white middle-class (heterosexual[9]) women had become the normative portrayal of women's subjugation. Hence one recent writer argues that "the same patterns of exclusion and marginalization that have been identified in traditional theology have tainted the liberationist project of feminist informed theologies."[10] Specifically, feminist theology was charged with "essentialism," though this was precisely what feminist theology had been trying to overcome. As Alcoff notes, whether woman was "construed as essentially immoral or irrational or essentially kind and benevolent she [was] always construed as essentially *something*."[11] To be accused of repeating this pattern under the banner of feminist theology was a hard pill to swallow. Yet

7. See Ada María Isasi-Díaz, *Mujerista Theology: A Theology for the 21st Century* (Maryknoll, NY: Orbis, 1996).

8. Kwok Pui-lan, *Introducing Asian Feminist Theology* (Sheffield: Sheffield Academic Press, 2000). Mercy Amba Oduyoye, *Introducing African Women's Theology* (Sheffield: Sheffield Academic Press, 2001).

9. The claims of heteronormativity in feminist theology are certainly not without basis; however, many second-wave feminists (theologians and otherwise) went on to advocate for a "lesbian lifestyle" as the only possible means of escaping the patriarchal reality. For instance, an early collective of feminist writers (including prominent theorist Sheila Jeffreys) argued in 1979, "We do think . . . that all feminists can and should be lesbians. Our definition of a political lesbian is a woman-identified woman who does not fuck men. It does not mean compulsory sexual activity with women." See Women Only Press Collective, *Love Your Enemy? The Debate between Heterosexual Feminism and Political Lesbianism* (London: Onlywomen, 1981). Hence this particular critique is complicated by the unarticulated notions of sexuality embedded in these texts.

10. Angie Pears, "The Problematization of Feminisms and Feminist Informed Theologies in the Twenty-First Century," *Political Theology* 7, no. 2 (2006): 222. See also Linda Alcoff, "Cultural Feminism versus Post-Structuralism: The Identity Crisis in Feminist Theory," *Signs* 13, no. 3 (Spring 1988): 406.

11. Alcoff, "Cultural Feminism versus Post-Structuralism," 406.

this challenge was important and necessary, lest feminist theology continue down the familiar road of objectification and oppression.[12]

At the same time, the ideals of feminist theology—equality, autonomy, and subjectivity—were being discredited in the wider philosophical schools. The libertine principle of equality, which had supplied the framework for the modern democratic state, was naturally an intrinsic feature of the feminist worldview.[13] A move toward the equal status of women and men was assumed to be a positive step forward in the struggle for women's emancipation. But exactly how "all men are created equal" was not originally part of the discussion. During these first decades of feminist theology, notions of equality were increasingly scrutinized to reveal the power structures that govern proposed social contracts and the manner in which the "masculine self" serves as an archetype for the liberal community.[14] The idea that all individuals could achieve the self-defining autonomy was found to be so laden with a Kantian notion of educated reason that "autonomy" could be simply dismissed as a bourgeois classism. That is to say, freedom and autonomy were seen as the result of a Western education typically pursued by men. Pressing further, French philosophical writers like Lacan and Derrida suggested that "the self-contained, authentic subject conceived by humanism to be discoverable below a veneer of cultural and ideological overlay is in reality a construct of that very humanist discourse. The subject is not a locus of authorial intentions or natural attributes or even a privileged separate consciousness."[15]

---

12. What's more, there has been an interesting attack on the whole enterprise of academic feminism, especially in regard to women's experience. See Elizabeth Fox-Genovese, *Feminism Is Not the Story of My Life* (New York: Anchor, 1996).

13. For an insightful and rather early account of the entanglement of feminist ideals within broader post-Enlightenment patriarchal systems, see Zillah Eisenstein, *The Radical Future of Liberal Feminism* (New York: Longman, 1981).

14. Serene Jones, *Feminist Theory and Christian theology: Cartographies of Grace*, Guides to Theological Inquiry (Minneapolis: Fortress Press, 2000).

These startling changes in the wider philosophical discipline brought a new set of challenges to feminist theology in considering women's emancipation and ensured that straightforward appeals to equality would be no longer possible. Yet perhaps the most significant blow to the fight for women's equality was the collapse of the category of gender itself. Secular theorists such as Judith Butler have undone much that was accepted as normative and stable regarding gender.[16] Butler's work regarding the "performance" of gender binaries and her efforts to destabilize such binaries has been enormously influential in feminist theology. Butler has argued (along with several others[17]) that we are inevitably culturally predisposed to a binary gender discourse.[18] Discourses around sexuality and desire are all formed to ensure that the heteronormative gender binary is kept intact. Instances of transgression (such as Freud's famous subject Herculine Barbin) are used by Butler to highlight the circular nature of gender binaries, and to demonstrate the essential flaw in such binary constructs; presumably a normative construct is incoherent if it ensures that a large portion of the population is considered abnormal. Categories that we might label with terms like intersex, gay or cross-dressing are not in fact examples of rule perversion but rather examples that demonstrate the flawed system. Gender can neither be reduced nor expanded to merely male and female. Gender, if anything, is fluid.[19]

---

15. Alcoff, "Cultural Feminism versus Post-Structuralism," 415.
16. Butler's most influential publications to date have been the following three books: Judith Butler, *Bodies That Matter: On the Discursive Limits of "Sex"* (New York: Routledge, 1993); Butler, *Gender Trouble: Feminism and the Subversion of Identity*, 2nd ed. (New York: Routledge, 1993); Butler, *Undoing Gender* (New York: Routledge, 2004).
17. For an excellent recent account, see Lisa M. Diamond and Molly Butterworth, "Questioning Gender and Sexual Identity: Dynamic Links over Time," *Sex Roles* 59 (2008): 356–76.
18. The term *gender binary* is referring to the categorizing of all humans into two distinct, opposite and unrelated terms of *man/masculine* and *women/feminine*.
19. See especially Butler, *Gender Trouble*.

Butler's work has helped feminist theologians to evaluate the construction of gender and how such a construction relates to faith.[20] However, Butler's theories also represent a threat to any sustained feminist theology. In rejecting gender binaries, feminist attempts to reclaim or revalue the particular identity of women seem redundant.[21] Add to this the fragmentation of appeals to women's experience (the critical starting point for the previous decades of feminist theology[22]), the intractable problem of essentialism, and the uncertainty about how to even frame the self or autonomy, and suddenly the enthusiasm for "sameness" in early second-wave feminist theology seems naive at best. What feminist theologians have instead discovered is a sea of chaotic and often conflicting narratives. The story of modern feminism is, as Susan Frank Parsons observes, the story of a developing awareness of difference.[23]

The Difference Difference Makes

No concept has garnered more attention in feminist theology over the last twenty years than that of difference.[24] The recognition of the importance of difference has been applauded as the "coming of age"

20. Nicola M. Slee, *Faith and Feminism: An Introduction to Christian Feminist Theology* (London: Darton, Longman and Todd, 2003), 110.

21. Susan Frank Parsons, "Feminist Theology as Dogmatic Theology," *The Cambridge Companion to Feminist Theology*, ed. Susan Frank Parsons (Cambridge: Cambridge University Press, 2002), 126.

22. Indeed many still argue that experience must form the catalyst for constructive feminist theology. See Margaret D. Kamitsuka, *Feminist Theology and the Challenge of Difference*, AAR Reflection and Theory in the Study of Religion Series (Oxford: Oxford University Press, 2007).

23. Parsons, "The Dilemma of Difference," 52.

24. For instance, discussions at the AAR are reported from 1991 in a session entitled "Appropriation and Reciprocity in Womanist/Mujerista/Feminist Work." Cited in Judith Plaskow, "Dealing with Difference Without and Within," *Journal of Feminist Studies of Religion* 19, no. 3 (Spring 2003): 91–95. Further, a roundtable was held by the *Journal of Feminist Studies* in 1994 in response to the infamous publication discussing antifeminism: Susan Faludi, *Backlash: The Undeclared War against Women* (Crown , 1991). In addition, the Britain and Ireland School for Feminist Theology Conference in 1998 was also on the theme of "difference."

of feminist theology, the entry of theology into a new arena of debate around matters of difference and plurality.[25] Yet feminist theologians continue to advocate for the importance of their discipline, even though the problem of the relation between feminism and difference remains unresolved. As Parsons says, "Something simply needs to be said about difference, and the difference difference makes."[26]

There have, of course, been a number of significant attempts to deal with difference while maintaining a feminist and theological framework. Serene Jones provides an outline of a growing group of scholars[27] advocating for a strategic essentialism:

> The strategic essentialist is a "pragmatist" or "functionalist," because she uses practical effect as the measure of theory. Instead of relying on rigid principles (either constructivist or essentialist), she asks: will their view of women's nature advance the struggle for women's empowerment? She also makes calculated, "strategic" decisions about which universals or essentials might work in a given context and which might fail.[28]

This response is both politically and pastorally charged. The appeal of such an approach for feminist theologians seeking to effect real change is obvious. Further, it takes seriously the critique of poststructuralism regarding the impossibility of a "view from nowhere." It creates a theoretical openness and a willingness to adapt to changes in the wider conceptual and cultural frameworks.[29] However in theoretical terms it does not avoid the use of power to categorize (and who has such power?) or the inescapability of further,

---

25. See Ann Brooks, *Post Feminism: Feminism, Cultural Theory and Cultural Forms* (London: Routledge, 1997), 1.

26. Parsons, "The Dilemma of Difference," 52.

27. See Diana Fuss, *Essentially Speaking: Feminism, Nature and Difference* (New York: Routledge, 1989). And Rosi Braidotti, *Patterns of Dissonance: A Study of Women in Contemporary Philosophy*, trans. Elizabeth Guild (New York: Routledge, 1991).

28. Jones, *Feminist Theory and Christian theology: Cartographies of Grace*, 44.

29. Serene Jones outlines quite helpfully the way "universal" approaches to women's emancipation has shifted over recent years. See ibid., 46–48.

possibly damaging constructs of women. As categories and needs proliferate, one must wonder about the effects of such fragmentation and the collapse of any collective or communal vision. The strategic essentialist still has to make normative judgements about woman and the nature of emancipation. Further, though strategic essentialism was originally proposed as a tool for intercultural dialogue and exchange, it is increasingly (quite problematically) favored as a theological tool for doctrinal exposition. For example, Nancy Dallavale employs a strategic essentialism to consider the sacramentality of "woman" in relation to the Catholic understanding of creation. In her account, a biological essentialism is necessary.[30] Not only does Dallavale reinscribe the gender binary as an essential element for continuity with tradition,[31] she pushes the use of essentialism beyond cultural and political negotiation and directly back into the dogmatic realm it was imagined to evade.[32]

Another important response to gender and difference within feminist theology has come from scholars seeking to incorporate the work of French theorist Luce Irigaray.[33] Irigaray affirms the otherness of the feminine and wants to raise the status of women's "semiotic"[34]

30. Nancy Dallavalle, "Neither Idolatry nor Iconoclasm: A Critical Essentialism for Catholic Feminist Theology," *Horizons* 25, no. 1 (1998): 23–42.

31. Ibid., 42.

32. Susan Abrahams has recently published a significant critique of strategic essentialism, with particular reference to the manner in which such essentialism seems "remarkably easy to co-opt for right-wing nationalist goals." Further, she observes how the early ideals of strategic essentialism have been lost in moves that co-opt strategic essentialism in theological anthropology. She notes, "Strategic essentialism as a category was significantly influenced by Gayatri Chakravorty Spivak's presentation as a concept to challenge Western feminisms historical complicity with imperialism. Spivak's understanding of the term, however, was in the context of cultural negotiations. Thus transnational feminist work not only identifies patriarchal institutional control of women but also explores the ways in which gendered, cultural, and political identity can be mobilized as part of a strategic proposal to patriarchy. Spivak never used strategic essentialism as an anthropological category." Susan Abraham, "Strategic Essentialism in Nationalist Discourses: Sketching a Feminist Agenda in the Study of Religion," *Journal of Feminist Studies in Religion* 25, no. 1 (Spring 2009): 161, 157.

33. Irigaray is actually from Belgium, but is commonly categorized with the French school of philosophy, where she has published most of her feminist theory.

or unique unconscious and aesthetic experience. In fact, Irigaray wants to challenge the entire Western tradition of phallocentric culture and to encourage woman toward a radical femininity. She claims that "the possibility of sex-specific cultural and political ethics is our best chance today."[35] By affirming embodiment (and bodily epistemology) and sexual desire toward the other, women are encouraged to pursue their *joiussance* and find themselves "anew, as subjects."[36] Many feminist theologians work within this framework. In the 1993 volume *Transfigurations*, essayists contributed to a discourse relating feminist theology to French feminist theory.[37] Tina Beattie is a contemporary scholar seeking to utilize Irigaray's thought within a Catholic feminist theological account of difference.[38] In dealing with issues of race and gender, Ellen Armour uses Derrida as a supplement to Irigaray in order to bring white feminism "to its end" and to respond to the challenges of difference.[39] Yet Irigaray remains troubling for the risks she takes in moving toward essentialism. Foundational feminist theologian Elizabeth Schüssler Fiorenza stands at odds with Irigaray's tactics, claiming that Irigaray wishes to "divinize sexual difference," while Schüssler Fiorenza's own agenda is to demystify gender constructs that are dualistic, heterosexist and essentialist.[40] Parsons defends Irigaray against these charges, and

34. Semiotic refers to signs and symbols. Irigaray argues that there is a unique semiotic flourishing within the emancipated woman, especially as the Oedipal structuring of language is exposed. See Luce Irigaray, *The Sex Which Is Not One*, trans. Catherine Porter and Carolyn Burke (Ithaca: Cornell University Press, 1985).

35. Irigaray, *Thinking the Difference: For a Peaceful Revolution* (New York: Routledge 1994), 6.

36. Irigaray, "Women-Amongst-Themselves: Creating a Woman-to-Woman Sociality," in *The Irigaray Reader*, ed. Margaret Whitford (Oxford: Blackwell, 1991), 190.

37. C. W. Maggie Kim, Susan M. St. Ville, and Susan M. Simonaitis, *Transfigurations: Theology and the French Feminists* (Minneapolis: Fortress Press, 1993).

38. Beattie argues that Irigaray "mimetically refigures the *persona* configured within the [Catholic] narrative in a subversive affirmation of the potential of Catholic symbolism for the creation of a culture of sexual difference." Tina Beattie, *God's Mother, Eve's Advocate: A Marian Narrative of Women's Salvation* (London: Continuum, 2002), 35.

39. Ellen T. Armour, *Deconstruction: Feminist Theology and the Problem of Difference* (Chicago: University of Chicago Press, 1999).

points to the openness of Irigaray's woman and her overall refusal to define woman. For Parsons, Irigaray challenges the easy alternative between essentialism and social constructionism.[41] Similarly, Diana Fuss argues that Irigaray is in fact teasing out the contradiction employed by Aristotle that a women's essential characteristic is to have no essence; for Fuss, Irigaray's employment of essentialism is strategic, a "lever of displacement."[42] Yet Irigaray is still extremely close to a heteronormative account of women that seems to rely on certain embodied experiences (especially sexual) for human naming and flourishing. Here lies the totalizing dimension of Irigaray's proposal. This becomes particularly clear as soon as one thinks beyond woman and the feminine—and it becomes clear too for any theological account that wants to affirm the dignity of celibacy. Regardless of whatever open-ended possibilities are imagined, Irigaray still sets up a strict boundary around "women" and proposes a self-definition that seems inadequate to the challenge of difference.

In short, what began as an enterprise seeking the equality of all women everywhere has become punctured by the very notions that first provided its impetus. This does not signal the failure of feminist theology, as some suggest,[43] but only a challenge that has not yet

40. Sarah Coakley, "Feminist Theology," in *Modern Christian Thought.* volume 2, *The Twentieth Century*, ed. James C. Livingston et al. (Minneapolis: Fortress Press, 2006), 437.

41. Parsons, "The Dilemma of Difference," 71.

42. Diana Fuss, "Essentially Speaking: Luce Irigaray's Language of Essence," *Hypatia* 3 (Winter 1989): 62–80.

43. Angie Pears describes the history of feminist theology as one of "fierce expectation followed by limited effectiveness." Pears, "The Problematization of Feminisms and Feminist Informed Theologies in the Twenty-First Century," 221. Though she fails to define her understanding of these terms, I would argue that this is an inaccurate reading of this brief period of intellectual activity. Consider a comment made by Elizabeth Schüssler Fiorenza. "I am often asked, 'With whom did you study feminist biblical criticism?' And I usually reply, 'Feminist biblical studies as an academic area of inquiry did not exist forty years ago when I was a student. Therefore, we had to invent it.' This question does not simply bespeak historical forgetfulness. It also reveals how far we have come in the past thirty years. I remember in the 1960s when I could read everything that appeared on feminism; in the 70s when I could still read everything in feminist studies in religion; in the 80s when I was still aware of everything published in feminist biblical studies; and in the 90s when I could still keep tabs on everything that appeared in feminist

been resolved. And notwithstanding this unresolved problem, it is necessary for the church to continue to engage with the critique leveled by feminist theology against the Christian tradition. In many quarters it seems very little has changed since the explosion of feminist theological scholarship in the 1970s.[44] Systematic theology is an apt example of a scholarly field that has shown little interest in issues of gender and has generally failed to engage with scholarship from women and from non-Western and nonelitist contexts. The same apathy can be felt in many pockets of the church; in many quarters there is still outright denunciation of any theology that would present itself as "feminist."[45] If a theological framework, feminist or otherwise, is going to account adequately for human difference, it would appear that a different course is required.[46]

Mistranslation: A Different Language?

It is significant that central to Irigaray's critique of Western phallocentric culture is her critique of language. Taking her cue from Lacan, Irigaray suggests that the entire Western system of thought and symbol is corrupted by a phallocentric desire to name and oppress the other. This system is so entrenched that women have no option but to create their own semiotic world with its own space to experience embodied life. This is not to suggest that women

---

Christian Testament/Early Christian studies. Yet, today, I find it impossible to be aware of everything published in the field. Feminist biblical studies have grown into an intellectually strong and healthy discipline." Elizabeth Schüssler Fiorenza, "Reaffirming Feminist/Womanist Biblical Scholarship," *Encounter* 67, no. 4 (2006): 362.

44. Issues such as women's ordination highlight this fact.

45. Consider the populist antifeminist rhetoric of Christian figures such as Mark Driscoll, Wayne Grudem, and John Piper.

46. It is worth noting that Angie Pears argues for a more radical contextual approach as a way forward, particularly in regard to seeking justice. I am not sure how much more contextual feminist theology could be. See Pears, "The Problematization of Feminisms and Feminist Informed Theologies in the Twenty-First Century."

can exist outside language games. Rather, Irigaray suggests, "in this division between the two sides of sexual difference, one part of the world would be searching for a way to find and speak its meaning, its side of signification, while the other would be questioning whether meaning is still to be found in language, value, and life."[47] Whether Irigaray's alternative semiotic is indeed possible is a matter of contention; yet Irigaray's critique of the ordering of language is potent, and theology of any vein would be foolish to ignore her analysis.

At the Britain and Ireland School of Feminist Theology Conference in 1998, Alison Webster presented a paper titled "Translating Difference: Lesbian Theological Reflections." Webster used the biography of Eva Hoffman[48] to stimulate discussion of the problem of difference. She suggested that the difficulty in providing an account of difference in scholarship may come down to issues of translation as opposed to issues of description. Webster suggests that when we draw from experience we are drawing on a multiplicity of changing categories. For instance, sometimes we may find it necessary to speak from a gender category, other times from a class or race category, and so on. We understandably select these categories as means of translation, and then go on to enact such translation in our language exchange. Webster observes,

> It set me thinking theologically about what we, as feminist theologians, are after through our encounter with difference. Is it merely to hear articulated an infinite variety of partial visions—or is it to bring these visions back together in some way? Are we in search of a common language? Or just dreaming of one? Or trying to create one?[49]

47. Luce Irigaray, *An Ethics of Sexual Difference*, trans. Carolyn Burke and Gillian C. Gill (London: Continuum, 2004), 126.
48. E. Hoffman, *Lost in Translation* (London: Minerva, 1991).
49. Alison Webster, "Translating Difference: Lesbian Theological Reflections," *Feminist Theology: The Journal of the Britain & Ireland School of Feminist Theology* 21 (1999): 50.

Webster provides no answer, but in reflecting on the problem of difference in her own life,[50] she begins to nudge toward a common language—and this may be precisely what a Christian feminist theology needs.

In my judgment, feminist theology has reached an impasse in regard to difference because it has largely failed to draw on the categories that give rise to its own discourse—that is, theological categories. For instance, in a recent monograph Margaret D. Kamitsuka has provided a lengthy exploration of "woman" in light of difference. In her 2007 publication *Feminist Theology and the Challenge of Difference*,[51] Kamitsuka argues for a retrieval of women's experience in ways that acknowledge race and sexuality in more transparent terms. Kamitsuaka seeks to offer theoretical tools that may "be deployed to face the challenge of difference for constructive theological purposes."[52] Along the way, she shows how postmodern, poststructuralist, postcolonial, queer, and postliberal theories help to articulate the problems and to define the human subject who is embodied, sexed, and different. She concludes with the questions,

> Is our analysis of selfhood, power, and agency full enough to be able to reconsider how normalizing terms such as these (and many other besides) might be reworked? Can the contested terms be negotiated, even appropriated, as feminist technologies of care that could foster a spiritual performativity celebratory of difference?[53]

Kamitsuaka's is a considered and thorough piece of constructive theory. She has clearly articulated the challenges to contemporary feminist theories (especially in relation to the problems of power[54]),

50. Webster's paper was a series of reflections on the varied relationships she has enjoyed and the categories of experience that matter or seem significant to each relationship.
51. Kamitsuka, *Feminist Theology and the Challenge of Difference*.
52. Ibid., 26.
53. Ibid., 158.
54. See chapter 4, "Theorizing Power."

and she employs hermeneutical moves to celebrate rather than flatten difference. However, by her own admission Kamitsuka seeks to "make the case for how a poststructuralist feminism that is attentive to difference can go forward productively in negotiation with the (patriarchal, heteronormative, etc.) Christian tradition."[55] That is, Kamitsuka has made a methodological commitment to contemporary philosophical theory, *and then* moved to integrate such theory with the Christian tradition. This is a common methodological strategy in contemporary feminist theology; the work of gender, analytic, and poststructural theorists has been decisive in helping feminist theologians to articulate the challenges and responses to the problem of difference. However, when this strategy is adopted, theology is unable to consider—not as a secondary matter but as a starting point—the resources of Christian theological language.

In this book, I will argue that Christian theological discourse provides both a common theological language that can reframe the conversation around gender and difference, as well as a subtly (yet radically) different way of formulating the question of difference. The questions I will raise in relation to Christian doctrine are fundamentally questions of discourse. Christian theology is discourse. God's self, God's revelatory acts, God's telos are themes that give rise to particular habits of speech. As Rowan Williams suggests, the theological endeavor is one of "forming a consistent speech for God."[56] In this sense, Christian theology is always pressing toward a coherent language of God and creation. Admittedly, the grammar of doctrinal theology may seem like a foreign dialect to the kind of feminist theology I have recounted in the preceding pages.[57] Yet I

---

55. Kamitsuka, *Feminist Theology and the Challenge of Difference.*
56. Rowan Williams, "Prologue," in *On Christian Theology,* Challenges in Contemporary Theology (Oxford: Blackwell, 2000), xii.
57. In this publication, terms such as *feminist theology* and *systematic theology* are often used. For the sake of clarity, some mapping is required at this point. First, feminist theology is a broad

hope to show that difference is first and foremost a question not of experience but of Christian doctrine. Many feminists will be uneasy with such an approach. I do not wish to suggest that appeals to individual experience render discourse a-theological; but I hope to show that doctrine can provide an alternative—and surprisingly rich and enabling—resource for feminist enquiry. I will argue that an approach grounded systematically in the tradition of Christian doctrine can provide theological coherency to otherwise unresolved problems of gender and difference.

Difference, Doctrine, and Discourse

Feminist theology has attempted to build its anthropology upon reflection on oppression. The importance of consciousness raising and giving women the power to speak cannot be overestimated. Yet in considering such tactics, it is fitting to question the kind of human experience that has been paramount in such feminist anthropology. By beginning with different human experiences, feminist theology was destined from the outset for radical fragmentation.

discipline that employs, at the least, a hermeneutic of suspicion in religious discourse. Such discourse is not necessarily related to the Christian tradition, and further, "feminist theologians" do not necessarily represent a confessional standpoint. The category of *feminist theology* as used in this book is meant to designate those theologians who are engaging, critiquing, and reconstructing the Christian theological tradition. There is no assumption made against confessional positioning (hence, post-Christians such as Daphne Hampson are most certainly included). Consequently, when categories such as *prayer* are discussed, I am assuming that whether confessionally Christian or not, a feminist theology aimed toward the Christian tradition would account for "prayer" as a matter of particular Christian theological discourse. Insofar as *systematic theology* is concerned, I am happy to contend with a generous and broad definition, such as that offered by Sarah Coakley: "An integrated presentation of Christian truth, however perceived (that's what *system* here connotes); wherever one chooses to start has implications for the whole, and the parts must fit together. However briefly, or lengthily, it is explicated (and the shorter versions, have, in Christian tradition, often been as elegant, effective, and enduring as the longer ones), systematic theology attempts to provide a coherent and alluring unfolding of the connected parts of its vision." See "Is There a Future for Gender and Theology? On Gender, Contemplation, and the Systematic Task," *Criterion* 47, no. 1 (2009): 4.

Methodologically, one might say that difference per se has had no anchor. I will argue that the discourse of Christian doctrine can provide an explanation not only of the goodness of difference but also of humanity's inability to navigate the challenges of otherness. This may seem an insular attempt to defend Christian territory; but that is not the intention of this publication. Indeed, I wish to show that Christian doctrine has its own resources of self-criticism, and that these resources can be an important part of a feminist critique of the complicity of Christian discourse in oppression and abuse. I wish to show, further, that such a doctrinal approach to feminist discourse is uniquely positioned to provide a means of articulating human flourishing, especially in relation to creaturely difference. This is not to suggest that I will ignore or merely contest insights from contemporary secular theory. Rather, I will aim for a more complex and fluid relation between Christian and secular discourse. Again, Williams is instructive here:

> Theology seeks also . . . to witness to the gospel's capacity for being at home in more than one cultural environment, and to displace enough confidence to believe that this gospel can be rediscovered at the end of a long and exotic detour through strange idioms and structures of thoughts. . . . But there can come a point here where the passage through unfamiliar media of thought provokes a degree of crisis: is what is emerging actually identical or at least continuous with what has been believed and articulated? This is a question that prompts further probing of what the "fundamental categories" really mean.[58]

Contemporary critical theory has made claims against metaphysics that cannot be ignored. And yet theology does not simply have to let other disciplines set the rules for discourse. Given that much contemporary theory is directed to discourse itself, theological method has been left in a puzzling state. What is easily forgotten, as

---

58. Williams, "Prologue," xiv.

Paul DeHart notes, is the way method in theology is "inextricably bound up with doctrinal issues."[59] Contemporary theoretical discourse often fails to understand the particularities of Christian grammar (what Williams calls the "fundamental categories" of doctrine), and is therefore unable on its own terms to resolve the matters that remain so problematic for feminist theologians.

I will examine three areas of classical Christian doctrine: the doctrine of creation, the doctrine of the fall, and the doctrine of the Trinity. Each doctrine is considered in terms of its explanatory power in relation to the challenge of difference. Christian doctrine tells a particular story of God, a God who creates and redeems, and I will argue that this story can inform a contemporary discourse about difference, and can reframe theoretical questions for a contemporary feminist theology. In exploring Christian doctrine, I will engage mainly with a range of contemporary theologians. My aim here is to stage a dialogue between the contemporary schools of feminist theology and systematic theology, each of which has tended to ignore the contributions of the other.[60] This approach will allow me to test the claim that Christian discourse has its own internal resources for exploring theoretical questions of difference.

In focusing on the particular doctrinal narrative of creation—fall—redemption, I am not concerned to develop a narrative theology, or to perpetuate the problematic notion that "God is a story."[61] Rather than seeking to claim allegiance to scriptural imagination in opposition to abstract metaphysical conceptions,[62]

59. Paul J. DeHart, *The Trial of the Witnesses: The Rise and Decline of Postliberal Theology*, Challenges in Contemporary Theology, ed. Gareth Jones and Lewis Ayres (Blackwell: Oxford, 2006), xv.
60. Of course, this publication will demonstrate how this is changing. For a helpful introduction into the ways in which feminist theologians are engaging more intentionally with classical doctrine, see Joy Ann McDougall, "Keeping Feminist Faith with Christian Traditions: A Look at Christian Feminist Theology Today," *Modern Theology* 24, no. 1 (January 2008): 103–24.
61. For an important critique of postliberal narrative approaches, see Francesca Aran Murphy, *God Is Not a Story: Realism Revisited* (Oxford: Oxford University Press, 2007).

my approach seeks to work with a broader sense of "narrative" and "tradition." As valuable as postliberalism has been in reconfiguring the role of Scripture in theological method, the approach taken here is one that accepts a wide network of "tradition" as important to claims of Christian identity and Christian discourse. Thus "narrative" is deployed in a somewhat ad hoc manner in this book, one that resists the temptation to locate a fixed and definite internal logic of the tradition. My aim is not to start out with an inflexibly consistent hermeneutical or methodological procedure, but instead to deploy a more flexible methodological pattern that I believe reflects something of the untidiness and complexity of Christian language and tradition.

Ninna Edgardh notes that despite the troubling status of difference in contemporary scholarship, to follow Christ is to be grounded in "the conviction that God, who is more different from us than anything we could imagine, takes on our own shape as a human being in order to make humanity change, and thus make us all different."[63] Though critical theory often garbles the particularities of Christian grammar, contemporary theology should give doctrine a chance to speak on its own terms. The argument of this approach is that the most potent and resourceful theological response to the challenging questions of gender and difference is to be found in a retrieval of a doctrinal framework for feminist theology.

62. A sharp distinction that George Lindbeck easily assumes. See George Lindbeck, *The Church in a Postliberal Age*, ed. James L. Buckley, (London: SCM, 2002).

63. Ninna Edgardh, "Difference and Desire—a Queer Reading," *Dialog: A Journal of Theology* 48, no. 1 (2009): 43.

PART I

Creation

1

Creatio ex Nihilo and the Nearness of Difference

To suggest that a Christian account of human difference would find grounding in the story of creation is hardly surprising. That a narrative about Creator and creation may say *something* about the multifaceted forms of human difference seems self-evident. However, feminist theology has been squeamish about the biblical creation narrative, not only because of certain masculine notions of the Creator God,[1] but also because of the particularities of male and female in the creation account. There is the difficulty of the Yahwist creation account in Genesis 2—especially the provision of woman to man—and the overwhelming binary force of the text, "male and female he created them."[2] The connection of feminist theology with

------

1. That is, the concerns frequently expressed around the image of "artist" or "craftsman" used to describe the creator God. Alternatively, birthing metaphors are still popular among feminists.
2. For instance, in considering the Reformers' understanding of the male/female creation account in the broader narrative of Genesis 2 and 3, Jane Dempsey Douglass shows how Luther (for the most part) took a step forward in attributing original equality between the sexes, but consequently uses the fall to advocate women's subjugation as the "express punishment of

ecological studies has given rise to an emphasis on more dignified accounts of the entire created order, while a concentration on broader scientific developments has seen a growing interest in theology's relationship with contemporary science, including scientific accounts of the nature of gender.

What is often assumed in these constructions is an interdependent model of the God/world relationship. There are two main strategic reasons for deploying such a model. First, in order to safeguard contemporary communal conceptions of identity, causality,[3] and even epistemology,[4] it seems God *must* be imagined in a way analogous to human community. That is, conceptions of God are required to maintain harmony and balance with the created order in a horizontal relationship that frees the divine from the oppressiveness of traditional ontology. Second, a God who is in some way dependent on creation is useful for synthesizing scientific discourse with theological language.[5] In the 1970s, David R. Griffin could confidently announce that "Christians have always needed (whether or not they have recognised this) a doctrine of creation that was consistent with the essence of Christian faith and the best science of the day."[6] The implicit enemy in these accounts of creation is the God of antimutuality—the naively Hellenized divine being of the creeds, as encapsulated in the doctrine of *creatio ex nihilo*. Though the *creatio ex nihilo* doctrine is rarely analyzed with much detail, it is roundly

women which must endure until the end of all time." See Janet Martin Soskice and Diana Lipton, *Feminism and Theology*, Oxford Readings in Feminism (Oxford: Oxford University Press, 2003), 87.

3. This is not only in regard to scientific postulations but also the questions of theodicy that preoccupy open and process constructions.

4. For an early example see chapter 5, "Knowing Nature," in Catharina J. M. Halkes, *New Creation: Christian Feminism and the Renewal of the Earth* (London: SPCK, 1991).

5. It is noteworthy, especially in light of open or process theisms, that models of theology that claim most interest in fluidity and impartiality are often harboring rather obvious priorities for propositional coherency, especially in an interdisciplinary approach.

6. David R. Griffin, "A Process Theology of Creation," *Mid-Stream* 1–2, (Fall–Winter 1973): 48.

rejected for the brutality and violence it has allegedly inflicted upon humanity, and indeed upon the entire cosmos. Thomas Jay Oord writes,

> The God whose unlimited power created something from nothing is capable of completely controlling that which God creates—which is everything. The God who can create *ex nihilo* is essentially capable of creating something from nothing in any present moment to prevent genuine evil. The God who creates *ex nihilo* is culpable for failing to control creatures or creaturely events entirely and/or failing to create instantaneously from nothing that which could prevent genuine evil. In short, *creatio ex nihilo* undermines a coherent doctrine of divine love. Christians should reject this non-biblical idea to affirm consistently the biblical claim "God is Love."[7]

In contrast to this approach, I want to argue in this chapter that *creatio ex nihilo* is in fact the most hopeful starting point for a Christian account of difference, and I want to show that feminist questions around gender are most fully appreciated and addressed from within the story of God's creative and re-creative agency. Beginning with the doctrine of *creatio ex nihilo,* and examining in particular the priestly creation account in Genesis 1—and its place within the Christian biblical narrative and tradition—will bring into focus what is at stake in the debate about creation and creaturely difference. Recent process-oriented attempts to account for difference and to liberate creaturely difference fail to consider the underlying grammar of the doctrine of creation and therefore miss an indispensable conceptual resource. For theology, the Creator/creation difference is not only the genesis of difference itself, but also the most viable place from which a broader redemptive account of difference may be developed.

---

7. William Hasker, "A Philosophical Perspective," in *The Openness of God: A Biblical Challenge to the Traditional Understanding of God*, ed. Clark H. Pinnock et al. (Downers Grove, IL: InterVarsity, 1994), 107.

Catherine Keller: Gender, Difference, and the Becoming of Creation in Feminist Theology

For feminists, there is at lot at stake in how society frames a creation metanarrative. It has implications, for instance, for the dignity of women's personhood within Christian communities. Ann Loades identifies four major barriers to affirming the worth of women in Christian theology: the failure to find femininity in God; the insistence that woman is derivative from and hence secondary to man; the assumption that woman is characterized by passivity; and the tendency to identify women with bodiliness as opposed to transcendent mind. In this diagnosis, Loades places particular blame on the creation account, or at least on dominant interpretations of that account.[8] Concerns surrounding the *imago dei* inevitably lead to further questions about the plight of creation and the destructiveness of dualistic or binary modes of thinking. Thus, feminist theologians have taken to reinterpreting the creation story. Coinciding with a growing concern for the health and future of the earth (in the aftermath of Lynn White's now infamous "The Historical Roots of Our Ecologic Crisis"[9]), many feminist reinterpretations of the creation account involve a sustained dialogue with ecological and scientific research. In recent decades, the feminist reinterpretation of creation has often taken the form of a pantheistic retelling—an approach that has reached its highest pitch in the sophisticated process theology of Catherine Keller. In order to show how these dual concerns (deconstructing the patriarchal account of creation and engaging with ecological and scientific scholarship) have driven this process-oriented approach with its concomitant dismissal of *creatio ex*

---

8. Ann Loades, *Feminist Theology: A Reader* (London: SPCK, 1990), 5.

9. Leona M. English, "Revisiting Voice, Subjectivity and Circles: Feminist Pedagogy in the Twenty-First Century," *Journal of Adult Theological Education* 5, no. 2 (2008): 112–25.

nihilo, I will trace the trajectory of feminist theological accounts that leads to Keller's work.

Sallie McFague and the World as God's Body

Sallie McFague's arguments pertaining to metaphoric language are well-known and bear enormous importance for feminist God talk. In applying her arguments to ecological issues, McFague developed parameters around postpatriarchal modes of representing the creative order. She writes, "It would appear that the appropriate language for our time, in the sense of being true to the paradigm of reality in which we actually live, would support ways of understanding the God-world and human-world relationships as open, caring, inclusive, interdependent, changing, mutual, and creative."[10] McFague exposed the limits and dangers of language for God—and of God's relation to the world—by showing how patriarchal systems of domination find footing in the language used for God and "His" relationship with the world. Of particular concern to McFague is the monarchical model for God's relationship to creation. McFague argues that the monarch God is inherently distant from the world (here McFague appeals to Kaufmann's "asymmetrical dualism"[11]). The monarchical model for God renders the world remote, perhaps even cut off from the divine. This model "supports God as a being existing somewhere apart from the world."[12] Certainly the metaphoric imagery of a king supports this claim. And McFague makes important links with the monarchical God and substitutionary theories of atonement. Further, she observes that this monarchical

10. Sallie McFague, *Models of God: Theology for an Ecological, Nuclear Age* (Philadelphia: Fortress Press, 1987), 13.
11. Ibid., 64.
12. Ibid.

God interacts only with humans, not with the rest of creation.[13] Here McFague points to the anthropocentrism of word-focused Protestantism (and interestingly, notes the various strains of the tradition that have asked for a broader cosmological view, even quoting Augustine on this matter). Clearly, there was a need for the theological tradition to take more seriously the ecological crisis of our age, and the anthropocentric emphasis that has dominated theological discourse. As McFague notes, any tradition that cannot include the whole world is sadly lacking.[14] Finally, McFague argues that the mode by which this God controls the world is a system of domination and benevolence. For McFague, such a God encourages passivity in humanity—a passivity that threatens the future of the earth in this "ecological, nuclear age":

> God's action is on the world, not in it, and it is a kind of action that inhibits human growth and responsibility. . . . No matter how ancient a metaphorical tradition may be and regardless of its credential in Scripture, liturgy, and creedal statements, it still must be discarded if it threatens the continuations of life itself.[15]

Though, as I will show, these two ideas—the monarch God and God's difference from creation—should not be conflated, McFague is right to point to the foundational underpinning of the patriarchal worldview in a specific interpretation of "creation." However, there is a distinct coadunation here between ideas of sovereignty and creative power. And this argument is made against a particular model, a particular way of reading creation and sovereignty. As McFague narrates her key critiques of the monarchical model (God is distant

13. This was certainly seen as an important challenge toward many "orthodox" descriptions of the God/world relationship, and concepts of ultimate redemption. McFague states, "[the monarch model] is simply blank in terms of what lies outside the human sphere. As a political model focused on governing human beings, it leaves out nine-tenths of reality." See ibid., 66.
14. Ibid., 67.
15. Ibid., 68, 69.

from the world, God only relates to human subjects, and God controls the world through domination or coercive benevolence), she also moves, without any particular analysis, to reject the doctrine of *creatio ex nihilo*. In rejecting monarchical metaphors (and rightly so, as McFague notes: "If metaphors matter, then one must take them seriously at the level at which they operate"[16]), McFague is likewise rejecting the traditional doctrine of creation: *creatio ex nihilo*. If McFague sees this, too, as necessary, there is a peculiar subversion of her own claims regarding the functionality of metaphor, and the need to reimagine ways of speaking God in our time (for instance: Are we to accept that concepts such as omnipotence and creative agency are immovably fixed and not *really* metaphoric language?). In moving toward a discourse of the world as God's body, McFague offers one response, but her argument fails to necessitate this as the only reasonable response; in fact, her response in my view is not imaginative enough: it has not truly deconstructed the metaphor of creative agency. And yet it has exercised enormous influence.

There are several moves that McFague makes in her reinterpretation that have been vital in the subsequent development of feminist creation thinking. McFague sees an evolutionary model of creation as a means of explaining origins. She sees this model as distinct from the kind of mechanical explanation that she associates with *creatio ex nihilo*.[17] Establishing such a firm binary between these two models ensures that transcendence is also at odds with the "reality" or "truth" of creaturely experience. There is an inherent self-evident logic to these claims in McFague's (re)telling of creation.[18]

16. Ibid., 65.
17. In particular, see ibid., 6–14.
18. There is an ironic twist to McFague's account of "reality." Claiming the obvious interdependency of creaturely life and God at a time when humans are suffering unprecedented isolation and increasing atheistic views highlights McFague's own arguments about subjective God talk and the dangers of analogous projections of the divine.

McFague moves toward viewing the world as God's body. She perceives this as a means of providing due attention to the symbiotic processes of life, and of affirming nature and embodiment in a way that the monarch Creator God never could. The idea of creation as God's body is, to McFague, far "less nonsense than the idea of a disembodied personal God."[19]

Catharina J. M. Halkes and the Resacralization of Nature

McFague's work was expanded upon in the creation theology of Catharina J. M. Halkes. In *New Creation: Christian Feminism and the Renewal of the Earth*, Halkes seeks to respond to the World Council of Churches' call for a reconception of the justice, peace, and "becoming-whole" of the earth.[20] Like many feminists, Halkes argues that issues of injustice, instability, and ecological disaster can be traced to the overarching paradigm of masculinity and dominion. Tracing the "masculine" through the centuries, she shows how technology (or the technological worldview) was a logical procession from the narrative of divine dominion cemented by the Christian (and masculine) creation account. Thus technology—the modern dominion of nature—is at heart a masculine attempt to order and control the creation. Referring to Bacon's "knowledge is power," and Descartes's "*maîtres et possesseurs*," Halkes remarks of the new nature paradigm, "In the combination of power and capital which this brings about, God's supremacy over creation is put out of action as a matter of principle. The promise of salvation must be realized through conquest."[21] And she adds that "the old mythical word

19. McFague, *Models of God*, 71.
20. Halkes, *New Creation*, 1.
21. Ibid., 77.

'subdue the earth' is fulfilled in technology. . . . For this reason we see in technology a glimmer of that first morning of creation."[22]

Halkes's thesis implies that the masculine interpretation of creation, passed down through the church, has proven the vehicle for the divinization of the masculine, while nature—understood as feminine—becomes fully the possession of the masculine. Halkes suggests that traditional accounts of creation within the Christian tradition have in fact severed nature's relationship with the divine. Christianity's representation of God's transcendence has "brought about an image of God closed in upon himself, in no way at our side, and far distant from 'his' creation."[23] In other words, God's transcendence has now become a sign of God's disconnection from nature, and nature has thus been desacralized and made the object of masculine control. This is an important claim for Halkes, as she goes on to argue for both the re-sacralising of nature and the re-sacralising of women. She takes McFague's idea of "creation as God's Body" and uses this as the basis for reconceiving immanence, incarnation, and creation.[24] Thus, for Halkes, life in God's body establishes dignity and freedom for women; likewise, the Eucharist takes on a deeper meaning, and she calls for women's presiding as a sign of God's presence in creation.[25] More clearly than McFague, Halkes articulates God's active involvement with the world; yet "the world, as the image of God's body, remains a risky image, namely, risky for God. It makes God vulnerable. . . . As risky as this image is, so vulnerable is God, and now we must add that this image also appeals to humanity, to our responsibility, to our will to be co-creative, redeeming and healing."[26] In making a connection back to the traditional account of

22. Ibid., 78.
23. Ibid., 86.
24. Ibid., 152.
25. Ibid., 153.
26. Ibid., 155.

creation in Genesis, Halkes describes her thesis as a dream in which "the chaos was still in motion" and "there was no thought of a God creating from nothing, as a hero, only by 'his' word."[27] It is at this point that feminist theology opens into a thoroughgoing process account that renounces entirely the doctrinal tradition of *creation ex nihilo*.

In forming her theological account of creation based on an interdependent understanding of the universe, Sallie McFague asked feminists and ecological scholars to make a choice between scientific coherency and transcendent models for God (without asking whether this dichotomy is real or may be contested). In her portrayal of creation as God's body, she gave Halkes the grammar of a panentheism that Halkes would come to consider as pivotal for "freeing" God from "his dominance and omnipotence."[28] Further, in both of these accounts one sees a certain Western binary understanding of nature—nature as the opposite of history, or nature as the opposite of humanity—being smuggled into the very project of subverting Western patriarchal logic. Such a sharp binary tends to force feminist theology into an impasse; the link between creation and redemption can only be maintained through a rearticulation of redemption that is far more radical than may have been originally envisaged by feminist revisionists.

The Face of the Deep

It is in the work of Catherine Keller that one encounters the most mature and comprehensive alternative to the doctrine of *creatio ex nihilo*. In *Face of the Deep*, Keller presents a complex rereading of creation, and brings together the many strands of thought seen in

27. Ibid., 154, 155.
28. Ibid., 156.

previous reactions against the traditional understanding of creation. Keller stands out not only due to the length and substantiveness of her work, but also because she explicitly describes her enterprise as a denial of *creatio ex nihilo*. In place of the traditional doctrine she develops what she calls a Tahomic theology—a theology of chaos and the deep. In *Face of the Deep*, Keller's earlier work on process thought, poststructuralism, and gender theory comes together in a work marked by engagement with continental philosophy and postcolonial thinkers, as well as "brilliant and unexpected interplays of biblical, rabbinic, literary, philosophical, astrophysical, and mystical citations."[29] Keller draws together seemingly contradictory resources into feminist scholarship, and more recent publications, such as Whitney Bauman's *Theology, Creation and Environmental Ethics*, continue to build on Keller's work and demonstrate the influence Keller now has in feminist thinking on creation.[30]

Keller begins by pointing to the obvious objections of locating *creatio ex nihilo* in the creation account of Genesis 1:

> This interstitial darkness refuses to disappear. It refuses to appear as nothing, as vacuum, as mere absence highlighting the Presence of the Creation, as nonentity limning all the created entities. It gapes open in the text: "*and the earth was tohu vabohu, and darkness was upon the face of the tehom and the ruach elohim was vibrating upon the face of the mayim . . .*" This voice evinces fullness, its waters, viscosity. It is no wonder that this verse got systematically forgotten, its own flood drowned out by the amplification of the first verse.[31]

Keller juxtaposes the *tehom* to the *nihil*, and argues for *creatio ex profoundis*; even as this account is shrouded in poststructuralist

29. Laurel C. Schneider, review of *Face of the Deep: A Theology of Becoming*, by Catherine Keller. *The Journal of Religion* 8, no. 4 (October 2004): 639.

30. Whitney Bauman, *Theology, Creation and Environmental Ethics: From Creatio Ex Nihilo to Terra Nullius*, Routledge Studies in Religion (New York: Routledge, 2009).

31. Catherine Keller, *Face of the Deep: A Theology of Becoming* (Abingdon: Routledge, 2003), 9.

sensibilities, one can imagine an entire systematic theology developing on this basis. Because of the importance of the rejection of *creatio ex nihilo*, Keller claims a direct biblical mandate for her reading of creation: the Bible "knows *only* of the divine formation of the world out of a chaotic something."[32] And conversely, "Biblical scholars cannot situate *ex nihilo* proper within Hebrew, Hellenistic Jewish or Christian scripture."[33] The exegesis here is decisive, as Keller knows well: "Among biblical scholars there has existed on this matter a near, if nervous, consensus on this matter for decades."[34] What are we to do with the abutment of the first and second verse of Genesis? It has been a question rarely broached, as Keller notes. And thus this meeting, the proximity of these apparently contesting discourses, becomes critical in Keller's exposition of chaotic multiplicity. Moreover, in reflecting on the motives for the church's development of *creatio ex nihilo*, Keller offers a historical account that traces the rejection of women, nature, and chaos in favour of patriarchy, transcendence, and order.

Suggesting that Hermogenes offered a protopoststructuralist reading of the khora, Keller shows that his subtle "third genre" would inevitably be repudiated in the aggressive binary logic of anti-Gnosticism.[35] This is a significant move in Keller's argument: not only does the biblical text provide contesting language in describing divine creative agency; the motives behind the antagonistic defence of *creatio ex nihilo* are considered to be primarily political. In reflecting on Irenaeus's *Against Heresies*, Keller suggests that the doctrine of *creatio ex nihilo* "has become so habitual, that we forget it had to be made."[36] Consequently, if Irenaeus's hands of God are

32. Ibid., 4 (emphasis added).
33. Ibid., 45.
34. Ibid., 4.
35. Ibid., 46–49.
36. Ibid., 50.

affirmed for reaching into matter, Keller is quick to remind us that Irenaeus is primarily concerned with arguing against multiplicity, emanations, and excess of any kind; he is quickly relaxing into a One that "strengthens the imaginary of unilateral, linear and masculine dominance."[37] For Keller, then, the gendered connotations of the development of *creatio ex nihilo*, and the vehement rejection of a potential *creatio ex profoundis*, must be expounded.

Keller's argument begins by drawing parallels between the face of the deep ("who was as far as we can remember—a woman"[38]) in the Genesis creation myth and in the *Tiamat* of *Enuma Elish*:

> Preserving the destruction of Tiamat as epic achievement, the *Enuma Elish* portrays the creation of the world from the hero's slaughter of the first goddess. Sanctifying the new imperial politics of Babylon, creation by war efficiently supersedes the trope of cosmic procreation. To this end the poet presides over the production of a most unfriendly face for the chaos. The *Enuma Elish* narrates the dramatic metamorphosis of *Tiamat* from loving mother of the gods to their direst enemy. The transition of the gender politics of the Bronze Age to an ever more central and patrilineal order [is] a transparent enough move.[39]

Although Keller agrees that Genesis 1 does not share the same fear of the deep, the inclination to matricide, or the violent urges of *Maarduk*,[40] she nevertheless argues "that chaos can never be dead enough," and that the *Enuma Elish* lies within the Genesis text as a prototype.[41] In making this link, and in calling for a retrieval of the wet womanly chaos, Keller naturally turns to the watery womb and finds there an alternative natal symbolism for creation. This ancient symbol has been banished for its failure to maintain proper

37. Ibid., 51.
38. Ibid., 28.
39. Ibid.
40. Ibid., 30.
41. Ibid., 108.

transcendence and is even under threat by feminists who seek to "dry her up" with concerns of anti-essentialism, antibiologism and antinatalism.[42] Here Keller wants to "destabilise colonized wombs" and to upset the phallic nature of *ex nihilo*. In the reinstatement of chaos, the body of God proclaimed by McFague and Halkes has now come into her fullness of being, or rather of her becoming.

For Keller, origin is finally abandoned altogether in favour of beginnings and process. Dynamism and vitality can only be understood in the "chaosmos" that Keller envisages. Though this is similar to McFague's association of origin with creation (to be associated with scientific process models), Keller wants to clarify the distinction between beginning and origin (utilizing Edward Said's postcolonial critique of origin theory[43]) and argues that any attempt to find an origin is an attempt to exert ontological control. This bolsters her conclusion that *creatio ex nihilo* is unbiblical, politically motivated, and ultimately, against human and ecological flourishing. Further, she suggests that Derrida's grammatology of beginnings is a far more appropriate conversation partner for the kind of Whiteheadean process thought she assumes in her project.[44] Thus Keller draws a Derridean "orginary trace" into the origin-free cosmology of process thinking as a means to explore and construct an alternative "philosopheme" of the deep. She writes, "Such a deep would signify neither an original presence nor a unified consciousness but a layered complexity, a multidimensionality of becoming, in which differences are neither kept separate (as in a clearly bounded dyad of Creator/creature) nor fused (as in pantheistic

---

42. Keller further insists that supposed feminist defences of *ex nihilo* exemplify the history of womb-annoyance or womb-avoidance among the tehomic emissions. Ibid., 223.

43. Ibid., 158.

44. Keller has previously defended this method, particular in her essay, "Process and Chaosmos: The Whiteheadean Fold in the Discourse of Difference," in *Process and Difference: Between Cosmological and Poststructuralist Postmodernisms*, ed. Catherine Keller and Anne Daniell (Albany, NY: State University of New York, 2002).

substance) but held in contrast."[45] Thus talk of creation is strictly limited, and theology is permitted only to address matters of becoming; *creatio ex nihilo* is completely excised from Christian discourse. Keller's account also renders history and soteriology superfluous. Keller not only expresses distrust of prominent accounts of history, or of the nature/history relationship (as in Halkes), but also challenges all systems of soteriology, arguing that soteriology necessarily abandons cosmological concern whereby "the creation founds and guarantees salvation."[46]

As Keller steps further back into the doctrine of creation to expand the narrative and to bring broader literary portrayals of creation and the cosmos into view, she articulates deep mythical foundations for a feminist discourse of creation. Yet it is worth pausing to ask if this impressive development of feminist theology has not evaded some of the fundamental questions and criticisms of feminism itself—questions relating to hierarchy, dualism, and essentializing. And what if this development has also failed to consider the doctrinal significance of *creatio ex nihilo* not only for patriarchal ordering and dominion, but also for their subversion? As I will contend, the secular riddle of difference is most fully addressed when the question of difference is situated within a framework of *creatio ex nihilo*.

Out of Nothing: Appeals to the Bible

Brian D. Robinette suggests that there are three prominent positions taken in assessing the validity of *creatio ex nihilo* in relation to biblical tradition. A first position suggests that *creatio ex nihilo* imposes something new and largely foreign on to the biblical text; in this

---

45. Keller, *Face of the Deep*, 164.
46. Ibid., 50.

view, the biblical text is subjected to an alien metaphysics. A second position recognizes the innovative character of the doctrine but also affirms its normative status in terms of doctrinal development; here a certain interplay between Scripture and tradition is regarded as a legitimate development. A third position argues that even if *creatio ex nihilo* represents a more technical conceptuality, it is entirely continuous with the content of the biblical text and in this sense is not innovative at all.[47] Though the third position may seem on the surface like a defensive reading of Scripture, the first two positions are in fact entirely dependent on claims about the exact meaning of biblical texts. Keller clearly adopts the first position based on her reading of Genesis 1, with little consideration of other biblical traditions or of the relation between biblical texts and their interpretive communities.[48] In what follows I will present a very different account of "the Bible" in regard to *creatio ex nihilo*. Instead of seeking to draw an overarching account of beginnings from the first chapter of Genesis creation alone, I will draw attention to the function of this myth within the particularity of the Hebrew Bible, and will further consider the thematic significance of "life out of nothing" in the context of the Christ event and the post-Easter community.

It is noteworthy that Keller draws attention to the "consciousnesses" of the Priestly writers in relation to other ancient Near Eastern texts, and yet she fails to make any mention of the writers' consciousness of the story of Israel.[49] The Priestly writers utilize the primal history to invoke the particular history of a people who begin not in a time of God's spirit hovering over the water, but in the event of the exodus. As Robert Jenson has argued, "In P

---

47. Brian D. Robinette, "The Difference Nothing Makes: Creatio Ex Nihilo, Resurrection, and Divine Gratuity," *Theological Studies* 72 (2011): 527, 528.

48. And indeed, Robinette cites Keller, along with John Caputo, as examples of this approach. Ibid., 528.

49. Keller, *Face of the Deep*, 108.

precisely the genealogies that stretch through Genesis 1–11 are the chief matter in that they establish a continuous sequence of events through the primal history to Abraham and beyond to Joseph and the rest, i.e., to the people of the Exodus."[50] If this is the critical consciousness of the Priestly writer, or rather the intent of their mythical text, then we should accept that the exodus is "the deed into which all the narratives of these people lean, even their creation narratives."[51] The whole reality of Israel is seen in light of God's act that summons the people and gives them their identity. Before the call of God into nationhood, and before the promise and covenant, there is *nihil*. The call and summons of God is itself the creative act, and hence creation is always cast in light of God's salvific action toward the people. This explains why *bara* is used mainly in texts that date from the exilic or postexilic period.[52] Rowan Williams points to the importance the exodus takes on in talk of creation in post-Babylonian exile:

> It is significant that such [creation] language seems to emerge into full prominence around the time of Israel's return from Babylonian exile (above all in "Second Isaiah," 40–55). This deliverance, decisive and unexpected, is like a second Exodus, and the Exodus in turn comes to be seen as a story of recapitulation of creation. Out of a situation where there is no identity, where there are no names, only the anonymity of slavery or the powerlessness of the ghetto, God makes a human community, calls it by name (a recurring motif in Is. 40–55), gives it or restores to it a territory. Nothing makes God do this except God's own free promise.[53]

50. Robert W. Jenson, "Creation as a Triune Act," *Word and World* 2, no. 1. (Winter 1982): 37.
51. Craig Keen, "Holy, Holy, Holy: The World Need Not Have Been" in *The Transgression of the Integrity of God*, ed. Thomas J. Bridges and Nathan R. Kerr (Eugene, OR: Cascade, 2012), 107.
52. David Basinger, "Practical Implications," in Pinnock et al., *The Openness of God*, 166.
53. John Sanders, *The God Who Risks: A Theology of Divine Providence*, rev ed. (Downers Grove, IL: InterVaristy, 2007), 67, 68.

So while we can clearly discern a link in the Priestly writer's connection between creation and the saving acts of God, creation precedes salvation in the sense that it is life, a sort of identity out of nothingness, that makes salvation possible. Indeed life out of nothing is a theme central to the entire Christian narrative. At the core of the Christ event one is forced to contend with the lifeless body of Christ, the pre-resurrection *nihil*. And yet on Sunday morning, the first morning, life bursts out of nothingness, calling all humanity into identity, to become a people in Christ. In Keller, the whole flow of this canonical narrative is interrupted, and the Genesis myth is made to stand alone, isolated from the historical communities in which the myth functions. Keller argues that creation is always incarnation, that it "would have been so without the birth of the Nazarene."[54] But here she ignores the particularly of Jesus the Jew, while also denying the Christ event its own narrative climax in the resurrection. Her discomforts about resurrection and *creatio ex nihilo* turn out to be closely related. Tellingly, it is not just some isolated bits of the tradition that get revised here; it is the tradition as a whole that seems to evaporate once the generative source of the tradition—an act of God in history that creates life out of nothing—is discarded. Craig Keen describes the indissoluble connection between resurrection and creation in scriptural tradition:

> When we remember the way Isaiah's soteriological vision grows and intensifies to give voice to a vision of God's unrestrained creation of the world, we may begin to hear in the Pauline passages (1 Cor 1:23, 28–30, 2:2, Rom 4:22, 24), which continue to live in the story of Israel, the hint of that most interruptive of creation pronouncements, namely, the *creatio ex nihilo*. Israel in Babylon faced a chaos that threatened its very existence. Jesus, the elect of the elect of God, was—the definiteness of the past tense must not lose its force—reduced to nothing. . . . The living body that had healed the sick and raised the dead was *an-nihilated* on the

---

54. Keller, *Face of the Deep*, 226.

cross; the dead weight of a lifeless corpse hung limply in its place. The entombed carcass of Jesus was not a latent potency waiting to be drawn to some entelechy. It was devoid of all "can"—in relation to the living Jesus, a pure nothing.[55]

Through a canonical lens, therefore, *creatio ex nihilo* is not simply a concept moored in a long history of philosophical debate regarding the divine; rather it represents an attempt of a particular historical (Jewish) community to come to terms with the presence of the risen Christ in their midst.

The doctrine of *creatio ex nihilo* is therefore validated not because Genesis 1 alone corroborates it, but because of a whole complex scriptural pattern that stretches from creation to re-creation, exodus to resurrection. This is not to reinscribe the kind of logos/lineal history critiqued by feminist thought. In the post-Easter account of *creatio ex nihilo*, the Christian church reflects upon a God who has engaged with time and timelessness, beginnings and ends, in a startling immanence. As Jenson puts it, "Linear and cyclical interpretation of our time [are] overcome by thinking of our time as encompassed in God's own life."[56] God is neither indifferent to time—collapsing our painful reality into timelessness—nor seeking to redeem time from outside the history of the cosmos. The Christ event at the center draws beginnings and ends and all of history into the creative (and re-creative) act of God. Jenson concludes that time "is the accommodation [God's] life makes in itself for the particular history that the Son in fact and freely is, Jesus' history with what is not God. Only this interpretation of time can makes sense of Genesis' assertion of creation "out of nothing.""[57]

55. Keen, "Holy, Holy, Holy," 117.
56. Jenson, "Creation as a Triune Act," 39.
57. Ibid., 40.

So while an isolated treatment of Genesis 1 will not justify the doctrine of *creatio ex nihilo* (though nor is the doctrine simply ruled out in Genesis 1, as Keller asserts[58]), a reflection on creation within the broader trajectory of Israel's history and the New Testament witness to Jesus the Christ uncovers the deep thematic pull of God's creation and recreation from nothingness. The abbreviated formula, *ex nihilo,* forms a coherent and, I believe, compelling claim about the way life and creation are understood in Scripture. *Creatio ex nihilo* cannot simply be dismissed as a destructive patriarchal move to impose order and deny the matriarch. It is "a post Easter narrative imagination, not unmoored metaphysical speculation," that underwrites the Christian discovery of this doctrine.[59]

The Closeness of Transcendence

The concept of divine transcendence is cast as the central villain in critiques of *creatio ex nihilo*. As advocates of pantheistic process models claim, what is at stake in this debate is the closeness of God and the dignity of creaturely existence. What I intend to argue in this section is that when transcendence is understood in noncontrastive terms it in fact dismantles the systems of combative difference about which feminists are rightly concerned. Difference from God and difference among creatures do not have to be understood as either a judgment or a threat. In God's radical difference we experience

---

58. Contra Catherine Keller, Robert Jenson argues that the purpose of the "when the" clause in Gen 1:2 is to make the creation story narratable. He argues, "The point is not necessarily to describe an actual state before creation; but if creation is to be narrated we have to start before it happens. Sometimes elsewhere such language works in that the pre-creation stage is indeed an actuality, which the Creator undoes or overcomes—as Marduk created by slaying Tiamat. But there is nothing like that in Genesis 1; pre-creation is described entirely by negations. Before God acted, there was only nothing—and 'the *ruach* of God.'" See ibid., 38.

59. Robinette, "The Difference Nothing Makes," 527.

God's nearness, and may come to know what it means to live as God's creatures.

That the God/world differentiation—as reflected in the articulation of *creatio ex nihilo*—was intended to have positive effects on the Christian view of nature and the self is hardly lost on feminists, though it is argued that this very move ensured the opposite effect, establishing oppressive hierarchies and destructive dualisms.[60] Perhaps this is due, as Brian Robinette suggests, to failures to radicalize the concept of transcendence in light of the Christian narrative, resulting in the kind of ontotheological claims that imagine God and the world to "coexist within a continuum and so relate on a competitive basis."[61] In the Hebrew Bible, however, transcendence is understood in relation to the unutterable name of God; God is the unfathomable not-I to whom we direct our worship.[62] Christian claims of a transcendent *and* Creator God hang together consistently when the sheer otherness of God is given primacy. As Kathryn Tanner notes, this means speaking of transcendence in noncontrastive terms.[63] The transcendent God who creates *ex nihilo* cannot be held in opposition to the creation—a creation that God inhabits in the incarnate Christ. As Tanner elaborates, Christian discourse must avoid "both a simple univocal attribution of predicates to God and the world and a simple contrast of divine and non-divine predicates."[64] Only by following

---

60. For instance, see Rosemary Radford Ruether, review of *Deconstruction, Feminist Theology, and the Problem of Difference: Subverting the Race/Gender Divide,* by Ellen T. Armour, *Theological Studies* 62, no. 1 (2001): 192–93.

61. Robinette, "The Difference Nothing Makes," 529.

62. For Keen, this encounter of Isaiah in the temple (Isaiah 6) exemplifies the recognition that "the shout of the seraphs is particularly excessive. It would have been already superlative had they announced that the sovereign is "holy, holy," that is, that this God is in every way other." Keen, "Holy, Holy, Holy," 111.

63. See Kathryn Tanner, *God and Creation in Christian Theology: Tyranny or Empowerment?* (Minneapolis: Fortress Press, 2005).

64. Ibid., 47.

this "rule," as she calls it, will God's divine agency evade the limits that render incoherent all talk of creator and creation.

By holding a kind of apophatic lens up to divine transcendence, we discover God's closeness to creation. "A non-contrastive transcendence of God suggests an extreme of divine involvement with the world. . . . Divine involvement with the world need be neither partial, nor mediate, nor simply formative: if divinity is not characterized by contrast with any sort of being, it may be the immediate source of being of every sort."[65] Such a grammar of the language of Creator and creation is important for reflecting on created differences, including differences of race and gender, and it is important also for developing a responsible ecological and cosmological account of creation in relation to a noncontrastive divine transcendence.

Divine power will also have to be understood through the lens of the Christian narrative. As Rowan Williams argues, creation out of nothing cannot simply be associated with an act of divine power over and something else; "creation is not power, because it is not exercised on anything."[66] The implications for feminists considering the *creatio ex nihilo* are enormous. The powers and principalities of this world, including the oppressive powers of patriarchy, cannot be considered analogous with whatever "power" means in the creative act; *ex nihilo* ensures that.

Moreover, in positing a noncontrastive understanding of transcendence, difference does not imply the kind of distance that Keller, Halkes, and McFague insist on. Rather, the more transcendent God is, the closer God is. For God is not part of the continuum of creation, and so is able to be infinitely near to all parts of creation. Creation inhabits the space of God's presence precisely through its

---

65. Ibid., 46.
66. Sanders, *The God Who Risks*, 68.

difference. As David Bentley Hart puts it, difference is right on the surface (not in the deep).[67] Instead of positing pantheistic models of the divine to secure some sense of God's nearness, the doctrine of *creatio ex nihilo* posits a transcendence in which God is freely and absolutely present to creation. Hart explains this paradox of closeness and transcendence in this way:

> Created difference corresponds to God, is analogous to the divine life, precisely in differing from God: this is the Christian thought of divine transcendence, of a God who is made inconceivably near in—whose glory is ubiquitously proclaimed by—creation's infinity of difference from God, its free, departing serial excess of otherness.[68]

But perhaps the most surprising conclusion is that the doctrine of *creatio ex nihilo* is far more adept than process theology at undermining the binaries and hierarchies that seek to define and categorize difference. Keller's project—by far the most ambitious and impressive of its kind—fails to deliver a genuinely fluid and liberative theology of *creatio ex profundis*. Does Keller's "natal metonymy of ocean and womb"[69] solve more problems than it creates? Can process thinking follow through on the ways a womb prevents or dispels life, or the instances in which the womb poisons the body? Though Keller repeatedly appeals to the subtle and sophisticated strategies of Irigaray to avoid charges of essentialism, it is still unclear that she has circumvented the binary of order and chaos. Rather, in the end it seems that Keller rejects order and reinscribes the feminine as chaos. This hardly encompasses the "queering" she refers to at the

---

67. David Bentley Hart, *The Beauty of the Infinite: The Aesthetics of Christian Truth* (Grand Rapids: Eerdmans, 2003), 180.
68. Ibid., 180.
69. Lisa Powell offered significant challenges to the womb metaphor in Keller's work in a session on disability studies at the 2012 annual meeting of the American Academy of Religion. This specifically related to the biblical notions of bareness and the essentializing Keller's models keeps intact.

start of her project. Critical questions aside, I have tried to show that the kind of process project that emerges as almost essential and inevitable in feminist and ecological accounts of creation are based on a profound misunderstanding and too-hasty rejection of *creatio ex nihilo*. To affirm *creatio ex nihilo* is to recognize the giving of God's self in the free gift of creaturely differentiation. "What God utters is God: the summons to the world to be, and to find its fruition in the being in the presence of God set 'outside' God and the kind of life that is God's."[70] Or in the words of Karl Rahner, "The difference between God and the world is of such a nature that God establishes and is the difference of the world from himself, and for this reason he establishes the closest unity precisely in this differentiation."[71] This doctrine at once affirms the dignity of all creaturely difference and maintains a transcendence that is neither threatened nor obliterated by the Other.[72] The binaries that govern and oppress much of the created order are transgressed by transcendence and immanence, transgressed by our difference and oneness, and transgressed by the Triune God's difference from all that is not-God. In God's life, differentiated creation is drawn into the one creative act, and called into identity and re-creation "in Christ." Rather than abolishing soteriology, a doctrinal account of creaturely difference welcomes the theme of redemption, not as the eradication of difference but as the gift that secures difference and rescues it from every threat, so that together all may learn how to live most completely and most fully in our differences—to learn, that is, what it means to be creatures.

70. Sanders, *The God Who Risks*, 74.

71. Karl Rahner, *Foundations of the Christian Faith*, 62, cited in Robinette, "The Difference Nothing Makes," 534.

72. Or as Eugene Rogers notes, difference is at the core of the perichoretic unity and love: "For God, intimacy is possible on the basis of difference. Because the three persons are distinct from one another, God can 'be' love; the relation of love can subsist among them." Eugene F. Rogers Jr., *Sexuality and the Christian Body*, Challenges in Contemporary Theology, ed. Gareth Jones and Lewis Ayres (Oxford: Blackwell, 1990), 198.

2

Creaturely Freedom and the Desire
for Selfhood

Contemporary theory is preoccupied with themes of autonomy, agency, and subjectivity. How are we to speak of the individual human in light of difference, and what difference does difference make to autonomy and subjectivity? In light of recent critiques of Enlightenment notions of freedom, it has become clear that any account of freedom must be constructed against the backdrop of difference and the space demanded for alternative conceptions of freedom per se. Moreover, a theological account of creaturely freedom needs to attend to the relationship between God's agency in the world and human freedom. This chapter argues that divine sovereignty must be the basis for a theological account of creaturely freedom in order to secure the coherency of Christian discourse. By locating creatureliness in the divine economy, theology is able to provide a rich account of the origin, calling, and telos of personal identity.

Groaning for Freedom or Turning to the Subject?

Freedom is a journey with others and for others towards God's future.[1] Freedom can never be defined once and for all. Freedom defined is freedom no longer, because it always transcends all our definitions or concepts. It can be experienced and celebrated only as it breaks into our lives as new awareness of hope in God's future, and new confidence in the growing ability to experience and share love with others.[2]

These words, written in 1974, are a reminder that freedom has been an integral motif since the earliest days of feminist theological reflection. The importance of this theme is hardly surprising given the many layers of women's oppression, both in stories of everyday life and within church rhetoric and ideology. In an extensive treatment of the fall myth in Genesis 3, Mary Daly wryly entitled her chapter, "Falling into Freedom," thus pushing the reader to consider both the oppression of Christian theology and the nature of women's freedom.[3] However, during the 1980s feminists across the disciplines began to question modern notions of freedom and the implications of utilizing such "freedom." In particular, an angry finger was pointed at Kant's representation of freedom. In her influential work on *The Man of Reason*, Genevieve Lloyd traced the association of reason with maleness, its development as a character ideal, and the way this notion of reason impoverishes both female and male.[4] More recently Reinhard Hütter likened Kant's free man to Prometheus challenging Zeus and becoming the benefactor to humanity.[5] In asking and indeed privileging the question "What is a human being?" Kant

---

1. "Groaning for Freedom" is a subject heading used by Letty M. Russell in her now classic feminist text *Human Liberation in a Feminist Perspective—A Theology* (Philadelphia: Westminster, 1974).

2. Ibid.,25.

3. Mary Daly, *Beyond God the Father: Toward a Philosophy of Women's Liberation* (Boston: Beacon, 1973), 44.

4. See Genevieve Lloyd, *The Man of Reason: "Male" and "Female" in Western Philosophy* (London: Routledge, 1984), 64-73 for an evaluation of Kantian autonomy.

makes philosophy "pre-eminently an investigation into the nature of man and assigns to it the task of discovering fixed universals behind surface differences."[6] It is not surprising, therefore, to find the affirmation of universal autonomy defended in light of Kant's ultimate aim for man: that is, for man to transcend heteronomy and the entanglements of dependency.[7] For Kant, reason is not only the vehicle of human freedom but also a form of existential truth. We are free when we demonstrate that freedom through our agency.[8] Strangely, such Enlightenment reasoning continues today in spite of the sharp critique of reason from feminist thinkers.[9] Though in the narrative of humanistic autonomy we may be led to believe in the godlike individual—who breaks free triumphantly from every constraint—what we in fact discover are the privileged freedoms of a social elite. In Lorraine Code's words, the ideals of the autonomous reasoner are "the artefacts of a small, privileged group of educated, usually prosperous, white men."[10] Sarah Coakley observes how

5. See Reinhard Hütter, "(Re-)Forming Freedom: Reflections 'After Veritas Splendour' on Freedom's Fate in Modernity and Protestantism's Antinomian Captivity," *Modern Theology* 17, no. 2 (2001): 117–61.

6. Michel Foucault traces Kant's development of this emphasis, a privileging of anthropology that was not found in *Critique of Pure Reason* but developed in Kant's later work. See Foucault, *Les Mots et les choses*, 352. Cited in Colin Davis, *After Poststructuralism: Reading, Stories, Theory* (London: Routledge, 2004), 129.

7. Sarah Coakley notably observes that this is Kant's response to Rousseau's romanticism. See Sarah Coakley, "Gender and Knowledge in Modern Western Philosophy: The 'Man of Reason' and the 'Feminine' 'Other' in Enlightenment and Romantic Thought," in *Powers and Submissions: Spirituality, Gender and Philosophy* (Oxford: Blackwell, 2002), 93.

8. This conception of freedom is tightly woven to Kant's notion of morality. Our autonomy is always reflective of our morality and vice versa. We assume something of our freedom (based on ontological categories of reason) in the same way as we assume ourselves subject to moral laws.

9. Here I am thinking particularly of the "freedom" presented in much of the literature associated with open theism. There is a painful irony in such accounts that suggest creaturely freedom is obvious in the common experiences of life—claims that are made so easily by white men such as Clark Pinnock. Thus when asked to justify claims for human freedom, he suggests, "The problem actually lies more in systematic theology than it does in religious freedom." See Clark H. Pinnock, "Systematic Theology," in *The Openness of God: A Biblical Challenge to the Traditional Understanding of God*, ed. Richard Rice et al. (Downers Grove, IL: InterVarsity, 1994), 105.

analytic philosophy is not adept at reading this subtext of Enlightenment reason:[11]

One may ask whether these enlightenment conceptions of "autonomy" continue to infect, albeit unconsciously, the incompatabilist vision of freedom promulgated by many philosophers of religion in response to the problem of evil. What difference would it make if this were acknowledged? It would, for a start, make it impossible for the promulgators of the "free will defence" to proceed as if incompatabilism were unproblematic in either gender or class terms.[12]

Feminist theology has largely moved on from talk of creaturely freedom. Discussion now focuses on the seemingly deeper problem of subjectivity, and confronting the possibility that there may indeed be no *self* in which we have invested our claims to freedom. The modern fascination with the self is well documented. Historians have traced the emergence of the forms of self-awareness we associate with subjectivity as a slow development. Colin Morris argues that what we now consider to be subjectivity began conceptually in the Middle Ages, and only reached its pinnacle in post-Enlightenment philosophy.[13] Yet in the past century, the concept of subjectivity has taken a savage beating. Martin Heidegger was notable in his critique of the assumed separation of subject from world. Ontological factors drove him to consider our experience of the world as a more pressing

10. Lorraine Code, "Taking Subjectivity into Account," in *Feminist Epistemologies*, ed. Linda Alcoff and Elizabeth Potter, Thinking Gender (New York: Routledge, Chapman and Hall, 1993), 21.

11. Galen Strawson provides an example of this within the analytic tradition. He writes that an awareness of self "comes to every normal human being, in some sense, in childhood." See Galen Strawson, "The Self," in *Personal Identity*, Blackwell Readings in Philosophy, ed. Raymond Martin and John Barresi (Oxford: Blackwell, 2003), 339.

12. Sarah Coakley, "Analytic Philosophy of Religion in Feminist Perspective: Some Questions," in *Powers and Submissions*, 99, 100.

13. Colin Morris's highly influential "The Discovery of an Individual" argues that in the year 1050 the social changes necessary for such a development began in European society. See Colin Morris, *The Discovery of the Individual: 1050–1200* (Canada: Medieval Academy of America, 1987).

question, and his insistence that the subject was a philosophical construct is still widely accepted.[14] Furthermore, in the aftermath of Freud's discovery of the subconscious a whole new set of factors demanded consideration in the pursuit of self. The politics of subjectivity became of major concern to an expanding group of scholars. Much of this political emphasis is credited to Michel Foucault,[15] but it is also true that a feminist reading of Freud's phallocentric model of differentiation brought about widespread suspicion regarding the ideal of personal identity.[16] Linda Alcoff writes,

> The self-contained, authentic subject conceived by humanism to be discoverable below a veneer of cultural and ideological overlay is in reality a construct of that very humanistic discourse. The subject is not a locus of authorial intentions or natural attributes or even a privileged, separate consciousness. . . . There is no essential core "natural" to us.[17]

Such a critical perspective is linked to the elevated status of freedom, and to the failure of the elite philosophers of modernity to consider realities dissimilar to their own. Indeed, "the revelation that the universal was in fact based on a distinctly male experience of selfhood galvanized feminist theory."[18] Further, while the ideals of freedom

---

14. Nick Mansfield, *Subjectivity: Theories of the Self from Freud to Haraway* (New York: New York University Press, 2000), 23.

15. Foucault is often read as completely deconstructing notions of the self; however, close readers of his later work argue that Foucault defends the subjective self and in no way abandons the self as previously assumed. See, for instance, Justin Infinito, "Ethical Self Formation: A Look at the Later Foucault," *Educational Theory* 53, no. 2 (2003): 155–71.

16. This criticism probably starts with Beauvoir's "The Second Sex," but reaches a climax in the works of Irigaray and Kristeva. See Simone de Beauvoir, *The Second Sex*, trans. Constance Borde and Sheila Malovany-Chevallier (New York: Alfred A. Knopf, 2010). Julia Kristeva, *Powers and Horrors: An Essay on Abjection* (New York: Columbia University Press, 1982). Irigaray, "Women-Amongst-Themselves: Creating a Woman-to-Woman Sociality," in *The Irigaray Reader*, ed. Margaret Whitford (Oxford: Blackwell, 1991), 190–97.

17. Linda Alcoff, "Cultural Feminism Versus Post-Structuralism: The Identity Crisis in Feminist Theory," *Signs: Journal of Women, Culture and Society* 13, no. 3 (Spring 1988): 415, cited in Eileen Schlee, "The Subject Is Dead, Long Live the Female Subject," *Feminist Issues* 13, no. 2 (Fall 1993): 2.

and liberty were seen as problematic to women and the poor within the West, such ideals are considered ridiculous on a global scale. As Kwok states, "The greatest irony of the Enlightenment was that the beliefs of equality, liberty, and dignity of human beings were used to justify slavery and colonialism."[19] Australian cultural theorist Nick Mansfield outlines the effects of this undoing of the Enlightenment ideal of subjectivity:

> I would have to say that not only do I not believe that an ultimate theory of the subject is possible, I also do not want one. It is the discussion itself that is of interest. It is worth noting that a genealogical approach, rather than a metaphysical approach to the subject, flies in the face of one of the oldest duties of thought in the West, the Socratic/Platonic command, renewed in the Renaissance and the Enlightenment, to "know oneself." In postmodern theory . . . this very command has been seen as destructive. Much contemporary thought aims to protect us from anything as definitive as self-knowledge.[20]

For feminist theology, this has shifted the goalposts, and has at times made a theological framework seem unnecessary for any feminist theological account of personhood.[21] However, two points emerge here as crucially connected to theological grammar. First, theological discussion of the human person is always a discussion of the created person, and is therefore always in reference to God.[22] Second, ideologies of freedom cannot simply be abandoned as passé or

18. Ibid.
19. Kwok makes this comment in critique of Rebecca Chopp's essay "Theorizing Feminist Theology." Kwok argues that Chopp fails to interrogate the racial prejudices that played into the modern constructs of self, reason, and history; despite this being the very theme Chopp is trying to deconstruct. Kwok Pui-Lan, "Feminist Theology as Intercultural Discourse," in *The Cambridge Companion to Feminist Theology*, ed. Susan Frank Parsons (Cambridge: Cambridge University Press, 2002), 30. See also Rebecca S. Chopp and Sheila Davaney, *Horizons in Feminist Theology: Identity, Tradition, and Norms* (Minneapolis: Fortress Press, 1997).
20. Mansfield, *Subjectivity*, 7.
21. Indeed the discussions of freedom, personhood, and subjectivity are themselves specialist areas of concern that can produce scholarship restricted to their disciplines, bearing little or no significance on each other. For example, consider models of identity in analytic philosophy and theories of subjectivity in continental philosophy.

irrelevant to the ongoing theological discussion of creaturely existence. In contrast to the scholarly rejection of the modern quest for women's freedom, public interest in this most coveted commodity remains high. As Linell Elizabeth Cady argues,

> Remembering it as the earliest version of feminism obscures the fact that it remains the most culturally diffused version, the one that commands the greatest respect and allegiance from men and women alike. This point is, of course, due to the fact that liberal feminism is rooted in the modernity ideology of classical liberalism, the primary language of American culture. It expresses its dominant vision in values, and hence a feminism grafted on to this worldview will, not surprisingly, be more widely received.[23]

In light of the so-called third wave of globalization,[24] the powerful relationship between communal economy and individual autonomy demonstrates how the assumption of human freedom is impressed upon a widespread global consciousness. Rather than abating, the ideal of freedom continues to expand within the two-thirds world. The free self presents layers of meaning that fall on both sides of the public and private sphere, and despite poststructuralist attempts to deconstruct notions of freedom, there remains a profound interest in the pursuit of freedom and the management of free people. As Kwok puts it, "Prominent economists have argued that all societies will have to adjust sooner or later to liberal capitalist modernity."[25] The literature of postmodern theory and the lived experiences of individuals and communities are in fact two sides of the one coin.

---

22. Or as John Webster suggests, "Because of the content of its confession of God, Christian theology does not have to choose between God and humankind, or to abandon both; passion for God is necessarily passion for humanity." See John Webster, "The Human Person," in *Cambridge Companion to Postmodern Theology*, ed. Kevin J. Vanhoozer (Cambridge: Cambridge University Press, 2003), 223.

23. Linell Elizabeth Cady, "Identity, Feminist Theory, and Theology," in Chopp and Davaney, *Horizons in Feminist Theology*, 19.

24. Here I am referring to the three-stage thesis of Larry Rasmussen.

25. Kowk, "Feminist Theology as Intercultural Discourse," 34.

To tease apart the self is to make claims about the freedom society imagines, and to speak of human freedom will inevitably spill into discourse of subjectivity.

Any theological account of the human person—a theological anthropology—will begin firstly with reference to God, and secondly will assume a direct correlation between concepts of freedom and subjectivity. But what has now become clear is that any account of freedom must be constructed against the backdrop of human difference and in relation to subjectivity, leaving space for alternative conceptions of human agency. When human difference is introduced as a pivotal concept within a theological framework, caution must be exercised. As Sheila Briggs observes, the yoke of difference is not evenly distributed.[26] Attempts to enforce an overarching paradigm of human difference may be nothing more than convenient tactics to ignore the particularities of oppression and exclusion. Systems and universals always walk a tightrope between provisional coherence and totalizing oppression. Yet the risk should not *in total* prohibit all efforts to speak of the human. On the contrary, the challenge of difference frees anthropology from tiresome campaigns to "round up" the human, and more importantly, reminds us we will not be able to speak of creation without speaking of the Creator.

Divine Sovereignty or Freedom Projected?

Theological anthropology commences with reference to God. Following on from the doctrine of *creatio ex nihilo*, it is right to start with God's sovereignty. The critical point that I want to argue here is that divine sovereignty is the basis for a theological account

---

26. Sheila Briggs, "The Politics of Identity and the Politics of Interpretation," *Union Seminary Quarterly Review* 43 (1989): 169–70.

of creaturely freedom, and that the coherence of Christian discourse depends in part on a conception of God's sovereignty.

The grounding of human freedom in divine sovereignty has been elaborated by Kathryn Tanner. In *God, Creation, and Christian Theology*, Tanner responds to the disintegration of Christian accounts of creaturely freedom.[27] She suggests that divine transcendence functions as a "rule" within theological discourse. More specifically, she suggests that, according to this "rule," divine transcendence must always be framed in noncontrastive terms. Conflict among Christians, she argues, "is not solved by further discussion of the subject matter in question, it is resolved by rectifying mistakes in language practices according to proper rules of Christian usage."[28] The particular locus for which Tanner makes this argument is the Creator and creation relationship. By carefully evaluating examples such as Irenaeus, Tertullian, Aquinas, Schleiermacher, Rahner, and Barth, Tanner argues that theological coherence is possible only where there is adherence to two basic rules: 1) God is spoken of as transcendent beyond any necessary relations of identity or difference with the nondivine; and 2) God's agency is spoken of as immediate and universally extensive.[29] As Tanner puts it,

> God must not be said to be at work to a limited extent on or with what pre-exists it. God must not be talked about as only indirectly efficacious of the whole in virtue of immediate agencies. In either case, God would take on the character of a finite agent; the rule of God talk as transcendent would then be violated. According to our rules, then, statements about God's transcendence imply statements about a direct and comprehensive agency of God.[30]

---

27. Tanner, *God and Creation in Christian Theology: Tyranny or Empowerment?* (Minneapolis: Fortress, 2004).
28. Ibid., 26.
29. Ibid., 81.
30. Ibid., 82.

Tanner argues that modern attempts to pair Creator and human agency have failed, or rather that modern methods "promote the distortion of both side of the rules." Theological discourse is coherent only where both human *and* divine freedom are articulated.[31]

Prior to making claims about the possibility of freedom in the face of human difference (as in poststructuralist concerns with subjectivity), Tanner considers God's freedom, and argues that divine freedom supplies a basic rule for discourse about human freedom. "The theologian must block the Pelagian implications that modern claims about the world and humans will suggest in talk about the creature's own capacities. . . . The theologian should stress God's sovereignty and talk of the creature with a constant thematic reference to God's direct creative agency for it."[32] To accept this basic principle is to take seriously the implications of a transcendent God for all other discussions about human beings or the world.[33] For while the modern tendency is to describe creaturely and divine agency as locked in competition, to reverse this trend and assert "I must decrease so that he might increase" would also be to misunderstand the meaning of transcendence. Our agency is not rendered moot in light of God's sovereignty. Theological accounts of creative agency and creaturely freedom are not a zero-sum game. As Robinette argues, grounding theological accounts of human freedom in divine sovereignty should

be embraced by anyone who wishes to avoid imagining God as a

---

31. Ibid., 121.
32. Ibid., 161.
33. In critiquing modern methods, Tanner goes on to emphasize that adherence to the "rule" cannot accept the modern tendency to understand "creaturely freedom as freedom from God, and creaturely competence as competence apart from the creative will of God." Or as she says later, in *Jesus, Humanity, and the Trinity*, "The distinctness of the creature is thus the consequence of relationship with God as its creator; her difference is the product of unity, of what brings together, of relationship. Tanner, *Jesus, Humanity and the Trinity: A Brief Systematic Theology* (Minneapolis: Fortress Press, 2001), 3.

whimsical power who intervenes here and there, or who violently breaks in upon the world in order to subject it to some implacable design. If God is regional vis-a-vis creation, the divine agency will also be regional, with the result that creaturely agency gains its autonomy to the extent that divine agency is uninvolved. Divine power, in so far as it becomes operative in a region where it does not yet reach, will do so in a way that extends, overcomes, appropriates, or cajoles.[34]

If divine and creaturely agency are not analogous—if they do not even bear comparison—then something more must be said about how such agency functions. In terms of causality, William Placher observes, "There is no independent causal continuum in which it is puzzling how God could intervene. . . . The only causal continuum is one whose every event God sustains. Divine action is not an interruption in or a violation of the normal cause of things, but precisely *is* the normal course of things."[35] Or in Tanner's analysis, "God's activity as the giver of ourselves need not come at the expense of our own activity. Instead the creature received from God its very activity as a good."[36] Karl Rahner describes this relationship well:

> This very difference is established by God himself, and hence something which is autonomous and which alone realizes this radical difference between God and creatures entails no limitation in God's sovereignty. For this difference is not something which happens to him, but rather he alone makes it possible. He establishes it, he allows it, he grants it the freedom of its own self-actualization of this differentiation.[37]

In short, human agency is grounded in God and is God's own concern, God's own gift.

34. Robinette, "The Difference Nothing Makes: Creatio Ex Nihilo, Resurrection, and Divine Gratuity," *Theological Studies* 72 (2011): 538.
35. See William Placher, *Domestication of Transcendence*, 190, cited in Robinette, "The Difference Nothing Makes," 541.
36. Tanner, *Jesus, Humanity and the Trinity*, 4.
37. Karl Rahner, *Foundations of Christian Faith*, (Crossroad: New York, 1976), 105.

Freedom as Gift or as Claim to Power?

If divine sovereignty forms the basis of creaturely freedom, theologically we can describe freedom as the reception of God's gift. Divine and creaturely differences, along with the differences we experience in our creaturely form, are grounded in God's gracious giving of Godself and of our freedom to be God's creatures. This freedom is always exercised in a particular historical context, a point that much theological anthropology misses. In response to the "death of the self" in postmodern literature, John Webster argues,

> The context in which a theology oriented to the Christian confession pursues its interpretation of human nature and destiny is a consideration of the economy of grace. What it means to be human can only be grasped in its full scope and integrity on the basis of a depiction of the gracious work of God, Father, Son and Spirit, in his saving self-communication with us.[38]

Webster is pressing toward the claims that all human life and history take place within the divine economy; human freedom unfolds within this particular context of dependency and grace. "The economy of grace is the history or (perhaps better) the drama in which God is glorified in the creation, reconciliation and consummation of humanity"[39] Webster defends what could be cast aside as a "unitary metaphysics of substance and presences"[40] because Christian talk of "human nature" does not denote a static or fixed *something* that hides behind the veneer of history. Such thinking, according to Webster, is "deficient because [it extricates] human nature from the temporal process of divine economy, isolating human beings from the unfolding drama of fellowship with God in which humankind acquires an identity."[41] When we talk of the

---

38. Webster, "The Human Person," 224.
39. Ibid.
40. Ibid., 225.

economy of grace, we recall the particular history of God incarnate; that is, we recall the gospel and the history to which it testifies. To do this is to speak of identity as the perpetual movement of receiving and responding to a gift. Identity, subjectivity, and freedom are all moments in which human beings receive God's gift and live within the drama of God's unfolding and sustaining grace.

What are the benefits of speaking of creaturely freedom in light of God's sovereignty and in light of the economy of grace? What difference might this make to debates about human difference? If freedom is to be grounded in divine sovereignty as gift, and if that gift is particular to the economy of grace, then—contrary to earlier feminist concerns—freedom is not closed off, it is not unitextual, it is not some *thing* that emerges in the projections of the powerful.[42] Such an understanding of freedom takes seriously the need for both theological coherency and real differentiation.

Here freedom is not being cast as unoriginated. This point is crucial in deciding how the debate of human freedom is framed. As Elizabeth Groppe notes, we live in a world "haunted by the ghosts of the fallen promethean dream of absolute freedom, a world wounded by our tragic quest for unorigination and troubled by the nightmare of determination by anonymous biological and economic forces in which freedom is either a complete illusion or nothing but a naked will to power."[43] The alarming questions related to power and self-determination, concerns that pave the way to the radical fragmentation of the self, arise not primarily because of modern concerns about divine power, but through the (seemingly

41. Ibid., 226.
42. Here of course my argument contrasts with the claims of Daphne Hampson, who suggested that a post-Christian feminism was indeed "breaking free." Daphne Hampson, *Theology and Feminism*, Signposts in Theology (Oxford: Basil Blackwell, 1990), 108–12.
43. Elizabeth Groppe, "Creation Ex Nihilo and Ex Amore: Ontological Freedom in the Theologies of John Zizioulas and Catherine Mowry LaCugna," *Modern Theology* 21, no. 3 (2005): 478.

empowering and benign) autogenesis of Kant's man of reason. Hütter argues that Kant's model "needed the cognition, exalting the self-posting of the 'I' as the ground of freedom itself."[44] In claiming freedom to be grounded in divine sovereignty and in the economy of grace, the will to power has very little to do with the givenness of our freedom to be creatures. If freedom is located in the grace-giving Triune life, all creaturely difference is freely opened up to divine difference and is invited to the experience of participating in divine freedom.[45]

From this distinction a second implication becomes clear. Freedom cannot be cast as prize or privilege. Debates about freedom and subjectivity are highly problematized when held in constant reference to combat and alienation (as in Lacan).[46] When theology appropriates this discourse, theological accounts of freedom miss the distinction of *creaturely freedom*. This is not to deny the complex factors that influence identity, human consciousness, and communal/economic ideology. Rather, it is to affirm that the free self—given in creation—has a particular origin and horizon within the wider frame of the economy of grace. The free self gravitates toward the Triune life. What it means to be a subject is not worked out in battle, defense, or subversion; rather it comes from grace and giving. In this sense, freedom draws difference together. Freedom is solidarity with the other, not privilege over against the other. It is here that one exercises one's freedom, as Kwok writes, by "begin[ning] to see the self in the other."[47]

44. Hütter, "(Re-)Forming Freedom," 125.
45. Groppe makes a similar claim in her evaluation of human freedom in the work of John Zizioulas and Catherine Mowry LaCugna. "Human creatures realise ontological freedom not by attempting to become unoriginal, a trinitarian property . . . but rather by receiving in gratitude our being-from-God . . . as an unfathomable gift." See Groppe, "Creation Ex Nihilo and Ex Amore," 480.
46. Nor is subjectivity the *no thing* that early commentators of Foucault claim.
47. Kwok, "Feminist Theology as Intercultural Discourse," 36.

Likewise, as I have noted, the freedom found in the economy of grace ensures that the subject is historicized. The failure of libertarian free will was not only the privileging of the Western white male, but also the cultivation of an almost archetypal picture of a free man. By moving toward a historicized approach, new categories of subjectivity become available to those for whom Kant's privileged model fails. In addition, such a move dedivinizes Enlightenment notions of reason. Linda Alcoff says of this historicizing of subjectivity,

> This will waylay the tendency to produce general, universal, or essential accounts by making all our conclusions contingent and reversible. Thus, through a conception of human subjectivity as an emergent property of a historicized experience, we can say "feminine subjectivity is constructed here and now in such and such a way" without this ever entailing a universalizable maxim.[48]

Such fluid conclusions may seem to threaten the stability of the Christian narrative. However, one can locate a doctrinal description of the self within the divine economy without forcing fixed systems at the level of culture. If human freedom is really a good gift, it will be open to the many contexts in which human embodiment takes place. Subjectivity is the occurrence of creatureliness within the particular history of God's gracious giving. Consequently, the contexts of community and culture will be understood as imperative for any account of subjectivity, but will likewise refer beyond themselves to the history of creation and redemption. Here freedom and subjectivity is not to be handled as a possibility only, but as the creature's living movement toward God and into God.

Rowan Williams once said that "being a creature is in danger of being a lost art."[49] Notions of freedom and selfhood have been muddied by the waters of modernity and postmodernity. It is

---

48. Linda Alcoff, "Cultural Feminism Versus Post-Structuralism," 430.

understandable why so many feminists have simply abandoned the ideals of the self. However, what I have attempted to show in this chapter is that, when framed by the Christian doctrinal narrative, freedom and subjectivity become thinkable again—not as something for which we must fight, but as the gift at the core of creaturely reality. We are free because we are creatures, and our freedom is a gift of grace entirely dependent on God's freedom. Human agency is therefore not in contest—not with divine sovereignty, nor with other creatures—but is sustained within the Triune life. As we learn, in gratitude, to receive this gift, we become conscious of God's history for and with us. Acknowledging our dependence and our call into the economy of grace is the means by which we ultimately learn what it means—for us, and for all others—to be free.

---

49. Williams, "On Being Creatures," in *On Christian Theology*, Challenges in Contemporary Theology (Oxford: Blackwell, 2000), 77.

3

From Twoness to Re-Creation

The Transgression of God

In Christian doctrine, God's creative act *ex nihilo* is held together with divine re-creation. This chapter will argue that one way of conceiving the re-creation is not merely as a secondary act to the *creatio ex nihilo* but as the undoing of binary constructs. This divine transgression is seen most powerfully in the theology and practice of the Eucharist.

Two Problems: Binaries and the Desire for Transgression

In charging traditional theism with a deep patriarchal ideology, feminist theology has frequently cited the oppressive nature of binary constructs. The domineering nature of binary thinking, and its destruction of difference, is often taken for granted in the vast literature seeking to unpack the various binary constructs that relegate whole legions of *others* to the margins. Gender, race, class, sexuality, and (dis)ability, along with many other hierarchically enforced categories,[1] are exposed as categories that serve and preserve the interests of the powerful. This exposure of power structures—with the concomitant recognition that language could be organized in radically different modes—has been the impetus for a whole generation of theologians working from the margins.

During the early years of second-wave feminism, it was the dualist worldview that demanded a response from feminists. Binary constructs and dualistic worldviews are closely connected, and it is difficult to tease these two epistemological devices apart. The history of dualism is usually described against the backdrop of Hellenistic philosophy, with Aristotle and Plato cast as the chief protagonists. Michelle A. Gonzalez remarks, "In the simplest terms, Plato's view of the sexes is grounded in his mind-body dualism. . . . With regard to their bodies, women are inferior to men."[2] Feminist theology has shared a consensus in condemning this system of division, especially for the way the entire structure of dualistic division is brought to bear on the experience of being "woman." Characteristics that have been held to be "natural" to the "weaker" sex—such as nurturing, empathy, connection to the earth, and contented embodiment—are

---

1. This kind of list is itself illuminated by Judith Butler as an example of the "feminist theory 'identity' list that leaves off with an awkward and embarrassed 'etc.'" "What political impetus is to be derived from the exasperated 'etc.' that so often occurs at the end of such lines? This is a sign of exhaustion as well as of the illimitable process of signification itself. It is the *supplément*, the excess that necessarily accompanies an effort to posit identity once and for all. This illimitable *et cetera*, however, offers itself as a new departure for feminist political theorizing." Butler, *Gender Trouble: Feminism and the Subversion of Identity*, 2nd ed. (New York: Routledge, 2008), 196.
2. Michelle A. Gonzalez, *Created in God's Image: An Introduction to Feminist Theological Anthropology* (Maryknoll, NY: Orbis, 2007), 19. As a more recent publication, Gonzalez's work takes into account the growing literature that suggests liberative aspects to Plato's dualism, especially when held in contrast to Aristotle. Both philosophers receive more sympathetic readings than early second-wave feminism, and their influence on Christianity is no longer simply demonized, as in the vein of earlier literature.

expressions of a lesser good, indeed symbols of a kind of fallenness. In 1983 Rosemary Radford-Ruther offered this interpretation:

> Both the Hebrew Genesis story and the Platonic creation story of *Timaeus* retain reminiscences of the idea of primal matter as something already existing that is ordered or shaped by the Creator God. But this now becomes the lower pole in the hierarchy of being. Thus the hierarchy of God-male-female does not merely make woman secondary in relation to God, it also gives her a negative identity in relation to the divine. Whereas the male is seen as essentially the image of the male transcendent ego or God, woman is seen in the image of the lower, material nature. Although both are seen as "mixed natures," the male identity points "above" and the female "below." Gender becomes a primary symbol for the dualism of transcendence and immanence, spirit and matter.[3]

Feminists have argued that such dualistic thinking thrived unchallenged into the modern period, and was bolstered by Rene Descartes's *cogito ergo sum*, with devastating implications for not only women, but for all of "nature" as well.[4]

Current concern over binary constructs represents specific questions pertaining to discourse and the ways in which language is shaped and performed. The charges leveled against dualistic worldviews are here taken to the particular level of discourse where semiotic systems are formed around binary constructs. Though concerns about binary constructs become prevalent only in postmodern literature, the advent of binary thinking is again traced to the fathers of Greek philosophy. G. E. R. Lloyd's historical account of early Greek thought traces the development of such dualism,

---

3. Rosemary Radford Ruether, *Sexism and God-Talk: Toward a Feminist Theology* (London: SCM, 1983), 54.

4. Carolyn Merchant published a remarkable study into the dualistic language patterns of early scientists. She examines the metaphor of earth/women awaiting scientific penetration, leading to the disastrous mechanistic view of nature typified in Descartes's writing. See Carolyn Merchant, *The Death of Nature: Women, Ecology, and the Scientific Revolution* (San Francisco: Harper Collins, 1980).

and offers three reasons for the emergence of dualistic thinking. First, many phenomena exhibit observable dualities. Second, the classification of phenomena may reflect and inform religious belief, which largely regulates society. And third, opposites provide simple frameworks of reference so that the "simplest form of classification is a dualistic one."[5] In poststructuralist literature, Jacques Derrida plays an important role in exploring new modes of thinking against the oppositional categories of binary logic. Rather than utilizing the metaphysical categories of sameness and presence, Derrida drew the contrast of otherness and absence into the conversation. These categories inform Derrida's belief that "reality is to be understood both in terms of difference, rather than self-identity, and in terms of perpetual deferment, rather than eternal presence."[6] At the level of discourse, Derrida's claims press deeply into language itself; in *différence*,[7] the endless potential for meaning exposes binaries as no more than movable constructs.[8] Derrida's strategy is best illustrated by extended quotation:

> The structure of the *double mark* (*caught*—both seized and entangled—in a binary opposition, one of the terms retains its old name so as to destroy the opposition to which it no longer quite belongs, to which in *any* event it has never quite yielded, the history of its opposition being of

5. G. E. R. Lloyd, "Polarity and Analogy: Two Types of Argumentation in Early Greek Thought," (Cambridge: Cambridge University Press, 1966), 80.
6. Eric Matthews, *Twentieth-Century French Philosophy* (Oxford: Oxford University Press, 1996), 168.
7. Graham Ward defines *différence* as that which "names the operation of difference and deferring which takes places among signs and which brings about a continual displacement or dissemination of meaning, and hence the supplementary nature of signification." See Graham Ward, "Deconstructive Theology," in *The Cambridge Companion to Postmodern Theology*, ed. Kevin J. Vanhoozer (Cambridge: Cambridge University Press, 2003), 79.
8. It is therefore not surprising that theologians have interpreted and engaged in Derrida's work in a number of diverse and even radically different ways. Stephen Shakespeare has very recently offered a commentary on these variances in which he notes the use of nihilistic theology, orthodox theology, radical orthodoxy, evangelicalism, mysticism, apophaticism, ecotheology and feminist theology. See Stephen Shakespeare, *Derrida and Theology*, Philosophy and Theology (London: T & T Clark International, 2009), 175–208.

incessant struggles generative of hierarchical configurations) works the entire field in which these texts move. This structure itself is worked in turn: the rule according to which every concept necessarily receives two similar marks—a repetition without identity—one mark inside and the other outside the deconstructed system, should give rise to a double reading and a double writing. And, as will appear in due course: a double science.

We will try to determine the law which compels us (by way of example and taking into account a general remodelling of theoretical discourse which has recently been rearticulating the fields of philosophy, science, literature, etc.) to apply the name "writing" to that which critiques, deconstructs, wrenches apart the traditional, hierarchical opposition between writing and speech, between writing and the (idealist, spiritualist, phonocentrist: first and foremost logocentric) system of what is customarily opposed to writing: to apply the name "work" or "practice" to that which disorganizes the philosophical opposition *praxis/ theoria* and can no longer be sublated according to the process of Hegelian negativity: to apply the name "unconscious" to that which can never have been the symmetrical negative or the potential reservoir of "consciousness"; to apply the name "matter" to that which lies outside all classical oppositions and which, provided one takes into account certain theoretical achievements and a certain philosophical deconstruction belonging to a not so distant time, should no longer be able to assume any reassuring form.[9]

Derrida assumes that language (and the use of language, especially at the hands of philosophers) requires a radical disruption in order to disturb the assumed metaphysical binaries. The false dichotomies of inside/outside and either/or reveal the manner in which texts construct and enforce the embodied binary, a reality which is itself equally textual. He goes on to claim,

Neither that of a reference (at least if conceived as a real thing or cause, anterior and exterior to the system of general textuality), nor that of presence in any of its modes (meaning, essence, existence—whether objective or subjective; form, i.e. appearance, substance, etc.; sensible

9. Jacques Derrida, *Dissemination*, trans. Barbara Johnson (London: Althone, 1981), 4, 5.

presence or intelligible presence), nor that of a fundamental or totalising principle, nor even of a last instance: in short, the classical system's "outside" can no longer take the form of the sort of extra-text which could arrest the concatenation of writing (i.e. that movement which situates every signified as a differential trace) and for which I had proposed the concept of "transcendental signified." Différence also designated, within the same problematic field, that kind of economy—that war economy—which brings the radical otherness of the absolute exteriority of the outside into relation with the close, agnostic, hierarchical field of philosophical oppositions, of "differends" or "difference": an economic movement of the trace that implies both its mark and its erasure—the margin of impossibility—according to a relation than no speculative dialectic of the same and the other can master, for the simple reason that such a dialectic always remains an operation of mastery.[10]

As with his critique of Western metaphysics,[11] much of Derrida's appeal to feminists (and other theorists writing from the margins) may be seen in the way he accounts for temporality in *difference,* and the openness this implies. In explaining difference, Derrida speaks of a third and fluid space that sign and meaning point to, and yet retreat from. The "middle voice" (a verb taking passive form yet bearing an active sense) becomes the means by which signification evades final meaning; or as Graham Ward puts it, "Deconstruction has a certain syntax that posits and denies."[12] In poststructuralism, not

---

10. Ibid., 4–5.
11. Of course, something must be said here of dialectical theology, which many proponents see as a means of overcoming pure dualism (or reductionism). Derrida's concern with dialectic methods is precisely with the desire for mastery the *Aufhebung* implies. Feminist theology has not generally utilized dialectic methods for similar reasons. As Peter Elbow notes, a major problem with the "Hegelian dialectic" is that in this form of dialectic, the opposites always "press on to a third term or a higher category that represents a transcendent reconciliation or unity: thesis and antithesis are always harnessed to yield synthesis." See Peter Elbow, "The Uses of Binary Thinking," *Journal of Advanced Composition* 13, no. 1 (1993): 52. On the level of creaturely difference—and with awareness of the ongoing relevance of identity politics—categorized human binaries are not objects to be transcended in order to reach some greater truth. Dialectics are considered in this regard far too violent an option for discourse that affirms the dignity of human difference in and of itself.
12. Ward, "Deconstructive Theology," 80.

only has the dualistic worldview been transposed into the linguistic structures of binary constructs, but it has also been given a way out, a third option. It is here that feminist theorists begin to speak of binary transgression. For Grace Jantzen, this concerns "dismantling the master's house,"[13] and for Ellen T. Armour the exposition of otherness in Derrida's work is crucial: "Derrida's textual interventions do more than uncover structures of meaning; they show that those structures of meaning depend on what they dismiss/define as 'other.' . . . Derrida gives voice to what is rendered 'other' by the text."[14]

No feminist theorist has done more work on binary transgression than Judith Butler. Butler's theory regarding gender performativity, perhaps her most influential argument, does not arise solely out of a Derridean framework,[15] although it is the poststructuralist project that brings the problem of binary constructs into clear focus. For Butler, "a restrictive discourse on gender that insists on the binary of man and woman as the exclusive way to understand the gender field performs a regulatory operation of power that naturalizes the hegemonic instance and forecloses the thinkability of its disruption."[16]

In the opening chapter, I have already touched on some recent responses to the challenge of creaturely difference, yet here I want to

13. Grace Jantzen, *Becoming Divine: Toward a Feminist Philosophy of Religion*, (Bloomington: Indiana University Press, 1999), 2.
14. Armour was in fact responding to Kevin Hart's claims that deconstruction could not assist feminist theory, as deconstruction is unable to take stands. See Ellen T. Armour, *Deconstruction, Feminist Theology, and the Problem of Difference: Subverting the Race/Gender Divide* (Chicago: University of Chicago Press, 1993), 71,72.
15. Most commonly, the psychoanalytic, and in particular reversals of Freud's theorizing, are credited in this regard. See in particular the early assessment of Freud in Butler, *Gender Trouble*, 78. However, as Kamitsuka argues, Butler most certainly engages Derrida's idea of words constituting a reality in an intertextual direction. Thus "inherent to any discursive performance is the '*citation and repetition*' of (con)textual convention." See Margaret D. Kamitsuka, *Feminist Theology and the Challenge of Difference*, AAR Reflection and Theory in the Study of Religion Series, ed. James Wetzel (Oxford: Oxford University Press, 2007), 70.
16. Judith Butler, *Undoing Gender* (New York: Routledge, 2004), 43.

spell out more clearly why theology from the margins continues to subvert binary constructs, and why I believe systematic theology has failed to consider the modes of repression that result from dominant binary discourses. Dualism and binary thinking are significant issues in relation to creaturely difference precisely because they impose seemingly immovable categories of gender and sexuality. For the white, educated, heterosexual man, the binary categories of which we speak are most likely welcomed, as they ensure stability, prestige, and power. However, those defined as other (women, black bodies, homosexuals) are relegated to the lower level of the hierarchy. For Beauvoir, woman was quite obviously the realm of the second sex.[17] Even more unsettling is the lot of those who fit in neither binary category: the intersexed person, the Asian,[18] the bisexual, or the asexual. For those who find themselves categorized as other, or perversely abnormal, the cost of binary thinking is all too real. As Butler notes, "The social punishments that follow upon transgression of gender includes the surgical correction of intersexed persons, the medical and psychiatric pathologization and criminalization in several countries including the United States of 'gender dysphoric' people, the harassment of gender-troubled persons on the street or in the workplace, employment discrimination, and violence."[19] The experience of real life binary transgression shows how violently such binaries are policed and controlled.

17. Simone de Beauvoir, *The Second Sex*, trans. Constance Borde and Sheila Malovany-Chevalier (New York: Alfred A. Knopf, 2010).
18. For a particularly insightful analysis of how Asian-Americans are "no-bodies" in prominent discourse on race, see Tat-siong Benny Liew, *What Is Asian American Biblical Hermeneutics? Reading the New Testament*, Intersections: Asian and Pacific American Transcultural Studies (Honolulu: University of Hawaii Press, 2008). Of course this is not only an Asian-American experience. The binary entailed by American white supremacy has led a variety of diverse voices to explore the ways in which "othering" binary discourse creates a multiplicity of "no-bodies." See Randall C. Bailey, Tat-siong Benny Liew, and Fernando F. Segovia, *They Were All Together in One Place? Toward Minority Biblical Criticism*, Society of Biblical Literature Semeia Studies (Atlanta: Society of Biblical Literature 2009).
19. Butler, *Undoing Gender*, 55.

Not only does binary thinking regulate norms, but it propels the ongoing habitualization and reenactment of the dominant categories. In fact, in Butler's account, performativity constitutes the sexed body.[20] Whether one wants to concede such ontological powers to "performance" theories, the uninterrupted power of reenactment seems a plausible description of the way bodies are regulated. Binary performance at the level of general discourse is particularly relentless. As Peter Elbow notes, "Binary thinking seems to be the path of least resistance for the perceptual system, for thinking, and for linguistic structures."[21] Though there is no doubt that oppositionary constructs are an "effective" way of sorting through data conceptually, what we are faced with here is structural power at its most basic level in the world of language.

The world of the binary is a world of twos; it is a world of the stable and the fixed. However, the Christian doctrinal narrative is directed wholly toward the Triune God who gently transgresses all supposedly fixed binaries, with a strange and inexhaustible threeness. Though theologians have a long history of defending dualistic worldviews or binary modes of thinking, the sources to which theologians appeal—as I now hope to show—turn out to be the very categories that bring such thinking undone.

Transgressive Re-Creation

Re-creation has been a critical theme in Christian theology. It is most commonly cast as a subsequent event in the divine drama, a second act of God intended to return the created order to its original state. However, the historical ordering of events in the divine

---

20. See Butler, *Bodies That Matter: On the Discursive Limits of "Sex"* (New York: Routledge, 1993), 140.
21. Elbow, "The Uses of Binary Thinking," 53.

economy is not necessarily the same as their theological order. Karl Barth notably proposed that "the Bible immediately compels us to consider the relationship between creation and covenant from a very different—indeed from the opposite—angle."[22] In reversing the order, Barth is able to argue convincingly that the love of God for the created order precedes creation's existence and is, indeed, the hidden reason for creation's existence at all. Later Barth wrote that "God creates, preserves, and over-rules man for this prior end and with this prior purpose, that there may be a being distinct from Himself ordained for salvation, . . . because as the One who loves in freedom He has determined to exercise redemptive grace that there may be an object of His redemptive grace, a partner to receive it."[23] Ignoring momentarily the concerns feminists might have regarding Barth's treatment of creation beyond humanity,[24] what we see here is playfulness, and indeed a certain fluidity in the ordering of things. *Creatio ex nihilo* and salvation, and all the categories we use to speak of re-creation, are not necessarily fixed by a binary reading.

In considering the doctrine of *creatio ex nihilo*, I have already made appeals to the Christ event as a means of understanding "life out of nothing." In the events of Easter, we come to understand God's creativity. Here the tension between creation and re-creation turns into slippage; just as re-creation helps us understand *creatio ex nihilo*, so too the *creatio* helps us to understand re-creation. As Craig Keen observes, "Because the *creatio ex nihilo* of Good Friday and

---

22. Karl Barth, *Church Dogmatics*, ed. G. W Bromiley and T. F. Torrance, trans. J. W. Edwards et al. (Peabody, MA: Hendrickson, 2010), III/I:41, 43.

23. Barth, *Church Dogmatics*, vol. IV/I:9, 10.

24. Interestingly enough, Valerie A. Karras has critiqued feminist eschatology for widening the lens in such discussion to include all of creation without realizing this is in fact still an operation of the western phallocentric framework. Instead she proposes to "reverse the direction in which the lens is pointed: from the created to the Creator." See Valerie A. Karras, "Eschatology," in *The Cambridge Companion to Feminist Theology*, ed. Susan Frank Parsons (Cambridge: Cambridge University Press, 2002), 248.

Easter Sunday embraces difference without indifference, it is an act of reconciliation—between us and God, and thus between us and all those entangled in the body of the resurrected Jesus, that is, the crucified Jesus in whom God embraces us all."[25] In the biblical witness to Christ's death and resurrection, the creation out of nothing is an act of re-creation, and vice versa.

In a fixed binary view, God's act of re-creation would be a response to the undoing of creation; the good is a response to the bad. In this view, God too is held captive to the binary construct; God must act, God must re-create in order to prove Godself to be God. The theological consequences of such a binary view of creation and re-creation are disastrous. Not only is God's freedom undermined, but the incarnation is reduced to a reaction rather than being seen as the fullness of the revelation of God. In Barth's account of creation, "God will redeem human beings through Christ, the Elect One, and in order to do this God will create the world."[26] Thus Barth's portrayal reveals paradox at play; though creation is the external basis for the covenant, it is also true that covenant is the internal basis for creation.[27] As Oliver Crisp argues, at the basic level Barth is arguing that neither creation nor covenant should "be treated independently of the covenant of grace."[28] Even if Barth was not concerned with binary constructs in his articulation of this relationship, his account demonstrates the way the grammar of Christian doctrine begins—even unintentionally—to subvert binary constructs.

In the divine economy, and especially in the incarnation, what is revealed is a God who transgresses binaries. The God revealed in

25. Keen, "Holy, Holy, Holy: The World Need Not Have Been," in *The Transgression of the Integrity of God*, ed. Thomas J. Bridges and Nathan R. Kerr (Eugene, OR: Cascade, 2012), 120, 121.
26. Oliver Crisp, "Karl Barth on Creation," in *Karl Barth and Evangelical Theology*, ed. Sung Wook Chung (Grand Rapids: Baker Academic, 2006), 82.
27. See Barth, *Church Dogmatics*, III/I:41.
28. Crisp, "Karl Barth on Creation," 83.

incarnation is the revelation of binary transgression. This means that it is possible to view re-creation—understood as neither the second nor the first creative act—as the undoing of binaries. This undoing is not the abolition of all categories, but the subversion of hierarchy as life is drawn into the divine fullness revealed in Christ. It is an apophatic undoing that neither sublates difference not essentializes it. It is a transgression that leaves us—where doctrinal discourse is in fact always located—poised delicately on the brink of heresy to the left and metaphysical nonsense to the right. And this transgression is most powerfully seen in the practice of the Eucharist.

Being Re-Created

To participate in the liturgy of the church[29] is to confess the presence of the Triune God. Moreover, it is to move toward or open oneself up to the new humanity founded in the resurrected Christ. Herbert McCabe suggested that "we can belong to the new creation, not yet physically but sacramentally; our bodies make contact, real contact, with the risen Christ through mysteries, symbols in which he is

29. The claims made here, however, have nothing to do with the ontological significance of the church. This is not an argument similar to that of William Cavanaugh, who suggests it is "the Eucharist which makes the Body of Christ." Nor am I seeking to argue that the Eucharist is the means by which God enacts a metaphysical transgression, a claim that characterizes various forms of Radical Orthodoxy. For example, Graham Ward pushes transubstantiation to the point that the Eucharist *is* the form of God's liberative action in the world. He argues, "For it is not that Jesus, this point, stops being a physical presence. It is more that his physical presence can extend itself to incorporate other bodies, like bread, and make them extensions of his own. A certain metonymic substitution is enacted, re-situating Jesus' male physique within the neuter materiality of bread (*to arton*). The 'body' now is both sexed and not sexed." In my view, it is precisely here that Radical Orthodoxy falters in its reading of the Eucharist. Ironically, despite Radical Orthodoxy's critique of modernity's atomizing of the subject, the actual bodies participating in the Eucharist seem immaterial. Indeed the ontological importance of the Eucharist seems purely rhetorical. See William T. Cavanaugh, "The City: Beyond Secular Parodies," in *Radical Orthodoxy: A New Theology*, ed. John Milbank, Catherine Pickstock, and Graham Ward (New York: Routledge, 1998), 182. And Graham Ward, "Bodies: The Displaced Body of Jesus," in ibid., 168.

present to us. In these same mysteries we are able to be really present to each other."[30] Despite the valid concerns of feminists regarding the sacraments,[31] the important factor theologically about the sacraments is that they are "about God, about what God has done and is doing, with and to the world, with and to us. We are called to be people who live through and in response to the creative and redemptive activity of God in the world."[32] And therefore the liturgical life of the church is fertile ground for the analysis of God's activity and our participation. It provides a means for us to understand God's life while having our own lives re-configured.

Alexander Schmemann offers a compelling argument to this effect in his classic text *For the Life of the World.*[33] He begins by suggesting that in the biblical creation account, human beings are presented as hungry beings who are offered the whole world as their food: "Man must eat in order to live; he must take the world into his body and transform it into himself, into flesh and blood. He is indeed that which he eats, and the whole world is presented as one all-embracing banquet table for man."[34] For Schmemann, humanity was therefore intended to take on a priestly role in both receiving the world and in offering it back to God. He continues,

30. Herbert McCabe, *The New Creation*, 3rd ed. (London: Continuum, 2010), xii.
31. The potential for women to preside at the Eucharist is sadly still a contentious issue in global Christianity, and presiding raises its own issues about gender and performativity. Bieler and Plüss show how the ritual reenactment of gender comes to play in the communication of worship. See Andrea Bieler and David Plüss, "In This Moment of Utter Vulnerability: Tracing Gender in Presiding," in *Presiding Like a Woman*, ed. Nicola Slee and Stephen Burns (London: SPCK, 2010). In contrast, feminists have also raised questions about the problematic nature of "receiving" the sacraments. In regard to the Eucharist, Natalie K. Watson writes, "Even if we kneel before God, the physical posture we are asked to assume can be reminiscent of having to make ourselves small before others." Natalie K. Watson, "Receiving Like a Woman," in Slee and Burns, *Presiding Like a Woman*, 141.
32. Watson, "Receiving like a woman," 141.
33. Alexander Schmemann, *For the Life of the World: Sacraments and Orthodoxy*, 2nd ed. (Crestwood, NY: St Vladimir's Seminary Press, 1973).
34. Ibid., 11.

> Centuries of secularism have failed to transform eating into something that is strictly utilitarian. Food is still treated with reverence. A meal is still a rite—the last "natural sacrament" of family and friendship, of life that is more than "eating" and "drinking." People may not understand what that "something more" is, but they nonetheless desire to celebrate it. They are still hungry and thirsty for sacramental life.[35]

Schmemann goes on to argue that the dualistic divisions, caused by the fall, ultimately drain life of its religious meaning.[36] Though Christ was the perfect expression of life as God intended (perfectly offered back to God), his death on the cross signals the condemnation of the entire world, and hence a re-creation is necessary. It is at this point that Schmemann draws attention to the eucharistic table. Though we already know that food is life, here we also remember that "we were created as *celebrants* of the sacrament of life, of its transformation into the life of God. We know that real life is eucharist. . . . This offering to God of bread and wine, of the food that we must eat in order to live, is our offering to Him of ourselves, of our life and of the whole world."[37] This same Christ, the incarnate God, the God who transgresses the binary, offers himself to God. The transformative depth of the Eucharist is seen in Christ offering himself, and in our recognition of Christ as Eucharist. Thus, while Schmemann begins by depicting the gathering of the people to participate in the liturgy—the work of the people—he reminds us that it is actually God who is at work, God who is doing something at the table, God who is creating and re-creating:

---

35. Ibid., 16.

36. Ibid., 18. Eugene Rogers makes the explicit link between pneumatology and matter (the spirit "befriends" matter) in relation to Schmemann. Rogers writes, "In Eastern Orthodoxy, as is well known, the Spirit so transfigures matter that the whole world becomes a sacramental element, an occasion for offering and thanksgiving." Eugene F. Rogers Jr., *After the Spirit: A Constructive Pneumatology from Resources Outside the Modern West*, Radical Traditions: Theology in a Postcritical Key, ed. Stanley M. Hauerwas and Peter Ochs (London: SCM, 2006), 69.

37. Schmemann, *For the Life of the World*, 34, 35.

In this eucharistic offering in Christ of all things to the One to whom they belong and in whom alone the really exist, this movement of ascension has reached its end. We are at the paschal table of the Kingdom. What we have offered—our food, our life, ourselves, and the whole world—we offered in Christ as Christ because He Himself has assumed our life and is our life. And now this is given back to us as the gift of new life, and therefore—necessarily—as *food*.[38]

God's power to re-create overcomes the dualisms that prevent humanity from offering the world to God, for in Christ the whole world is restored and humanity is made one again. The world which was separated into segments of opposing categories finds itself re-created and restored, and in this restored world humanity is restored to its priestly function through the high priesthood of Christ.

The priestly function thus offers a profound picture of binary transgression. Sarah Coakley provides an illuminating reflection on this work of re-creation. In developing a speculative argument around the nature of priesthood and gender identification, Coakley uses the Christ/church nuptial metaphor to examine the priest at the altar. However, the crux of her argument comes from her own experience of the priesthood, and her recognition of the need to make theological choices regarding the "intuitive category of ritual performance."[39] In particular, she reflects on the experience of celebrating the Eucharist in the east-facing position:

When the priest has her back to the people, it is symbolically clear that she is adopting the position of "offering" on behalf of the laity: she is facing Godwards, representing the *laos*. In the terms of the old "natural signs," the priest is "feminine" in this posture—supremely Marian, as Balthasar would see it. But when she turns around, whether to greet (at the *sursum corda*), or to offer the consecrated elements, or to bless, she has moved to the other side of the divine, representing Christ,

38. Ibid., 41.
39. Sarah Coakley, "The Woman at the Altar: Cosmological Disturbance of Gender Subversion?," *Anglican Theological Review* 86, no. 1 (2004): 76.

offering God to the people—again, in the terms of the nuptial metaphor, both summoning and destabilising the "masculine" posture of the bridegroom's self gift. Without these bodily reversals and movements in the liturgy, . . . something deeply significant to the enactment of this destabilisation is lost.[40]

Coakley argues that while these reversals have always taken place, the woman priest most vividly exposes the destabilization of binaries that occurs in the liturgy. The woman priest gestures "to the endlessness of the movement of gender subversion between the divine and the human."[41] This is not to be understood as a performance exclusive to the priest, since elsewhere Coakley argues that in the Eucharist "the priest as much as the 'layperson'" performs this role of "a Christic person."[42] Like Schmemann, Coakley sees the priest being drawn into God's transgression of binaries in the Eucharistic re-creation. If the kind of cosmological disturbance (the transgression of binaries) that Coakley imagines in the Eucharist is indeed taking place—a disturbance that re-orders the world—then it seems there is in fact nothing more poignant or more appropriate than the black woman at the altar, or the gay man, or the intersexed body. And the eucharistic transgression does not result in some new androgynous stability; there is rather an endless movement of fluidity and slippage that shows the subtle yet radical miracle of divine enfleshment and divine re-creation challenging and undercutting the "rigid orderings of the world."

Ultimately, like Schmemann, Coakley points not to what the priest enacts, but to God's action on the priest, and indeed upon the whole of creation. As she concludes, "Insofar as the world is thus re-ordered, we know that the Spirit has broken in, and the Word made flesh;

---

40. Ibid., 89.

41. Ibid., 90.

42. Rupert Shortt, *God's Advocates: Christian Thinkers in Conversation* (London: Darton Longman & Todd, 2005), 80.

for what, after all, is the Incarnation itself, if not the greatest 'cosmological disturbance' that the 'world' has known?"[43]

43. Coakley, "The Woman at the Altar," 93.

PART II

Fall

4

———

Original Sin

Prayer, the Presence of God, and Sin Interrupted

The doctrine of creation is at the core of any theological discussion regarding human difference. Theological distinctions regarding creaturely freedom and divine sovereignty are not always appreciated, and a tendency toward ontotheological categories can easily distort the divine and creaturely relationship. A Christian theological account of difference is most fertile and coherent when divine transcendence is understood to affirm the goodness of God's creation and to challenge contemporary theoretical accounts of power and autonomy. However, theological accounts must also attend to the doctrinal language of the fall and original sin; otherwise whatever else we have said about creation will be less than adequate. Far from being bad news for feminists, the doctrine of original sin, I want to argue, opens space to reconfigure theological debate around power and difference.

From the earliest days of second-wave feminism, feminist theologians have expressed concern, to put it mildly, about traditional accounts of original sin. In considering the tangled web of metaphysics, sexuality, and the idea of a hereditary transmission of guilt, it is not difficult to sympathize with the feminist inclination to denounce this doctrine of Christian faith. In this chapter I will reconsider the doctrine of original sin as depicted in Augustine's *Confessions,* and will argue that a theology of sin provides important insights into creaturely difference. The idea of original sin, when placed within the Christian account of creation and redemption, ensures that creaturely difference is held together in solidarity and not cast into permanent fragmentation. While contemporary theory offers insight into the mechanics and structural interplay of oppression and abuse, the doctrine of original sin belongs to a metanarrative that can speak to all "wrongdoing," in all manner of contextualized/historicized manifestations, while holding together all contesting accounts of human identity. Within Christian doctrinal grammar, it is the function of this doctrine to provide a theological account of evil and responsibility while maintaining an open space for difference.

The Sin of the Fathers

It is clear that many of the characteristic emphases of contemporary theology—its definition of the human situation in terms of anxiety, estrangement, and the conflict between necessity and freedom; its identification of sin with pride, will-to-power, exploitation, self-assertiveness, and the treatment of others as objects rather than persons; its conception of redemption as restoring *to man* what he fundamentally lacks . . . —it is clear that such an analysis of man's dilemma was profoundly responsive and relevant to the concrete facts of *modern man's experience.* . . . This theology is not adequate to the human situation;

its inadequacy is clear to no one more than to certain contemporary women.[1]

There is no doubt that feminist theologians continue to resonate with Valerie Saiving's words despite the monumental changes in questions posed by feminist scholarship. As long as *superbia*—and the anxiety arising from self-indulgence—remains dominant in the rhetoric of sin, feminist theologians will protest against sin on behalf of creaturely difference. Sin is often noted as the "one doctrine more than any other that has served to legitimize and perpetuate the oppression of women."[2] In addition to being condemned for an agency many women simply did not possess, women frequently reported the pedagogical experience of learning original sin as a process of learning that one's body and sexuality are essentially bad.[3] Consequently, feminist theologians have constructed a variety of alternative accounts for sin, seeking methods to abandon the masculine paradigm of sin.[4] In 1983, Rosemary Radford Ruether defined sexism as sin, and made the claim that patriarchy was in fact the original sin.[5] In turn, Reuther's claim was critiqued and expanded upon in light of race, particularly in the work of Delores Williams. For Williams, the white woman's account of sin failed

1. Valerie Saiving, "The Human Situation: A Feminine View," *Journal of Religion* 40 (April 1960): 107. Emphasis added.
2. Derek R. Nelson, *What's Wrong with Sin* (New York: T & T Clark, 2009), 115.
3. For instance, Serene Jones reports this common assertion in study groups. See Jones, *Feminist Theory and Christian Theology: Cartographies of Grace*, Guides to Theological Inquiry (Minneapolis: Fortress Press, 2000), 94.
4. A common move is simply to critique the doctrine of original sin for its negativity. For instance, when raising the question of difference, Gloria Albrecht criticizes Stanley Hauerwas for an extremely pessimistic anthropology. And thus, for Albrecht sin is a matter of limits and not 'morality." Therefore she critiques Augustine for emphasizing human guilt as opposed to accepting the limits of human powers. See Gloria H. Albrecht, "Unmasking the Differences: Nonviolence and Social Control," *Cross Currents* 52, no. 1 (2002): 25 and 18.
5. Ruether, *Sexism and God-Talk: Toward a Feminist Theology* (London: SCM, 1983). Certainly Ruether has gone onto develop and nuance her account of sin and original sin through a number of publications. Derek R. Nelson provides a helpful account of Ruther's work on "sin" in Nelson, *What's Wrong with Sin*, 146–45.

to consider the web of economic and racial factors that speak to "women's experience"—a move that relegated poor black women to the "underside of the underside."[6] Sin, Williams argued, should be spoken of in terms of racist gender oppression.[7] Not surprisingly, these anthropocentric descriptions of sin were also challenged when Sallie McFague placed sin talk at the center of ecological disaster.[8]

During the last three decades, feminist theology has gone on to challenge the highly individualistic and spiritualized accounts of sin that have assumed dominance. In her influential essay *Evil, Sin, and Violation of the Vulnerable,* Mary Potter Engel invoked the category of evil to claim that "it is not superpersonal forces but structures of oppression, patterns larger than individuals and groups . . . that tempt us toward injustice and piety—social, political, economic arrangements that distort our perceptions or restrain our abilities to such an extent that we find it difficult to choose or do good."[9] The liberation motifs of structural and systemic sin have proven a very helpful way to consider the relation between sin and difference. In condemning the dominant structures of white male power, feminist theologians have been able to articulate more specifically the ways social sin has "required that social groups be in the role of the despised or the defiled Other."[10] Hence ethnicity, sexuality, ableism, gender, religion, and many other expressions of human difference must be considered in accounts of societal sin.

6. Delores Williams, *Sisters in the Wilderness: The Challenge of Womanist God-Talk,* (Maryknoll, NY: Orbis, 1993), 144.
7. Williams, "The Color of Feminism, or: Speaking the Black Woman's Tongue," in *Feminist Theological Ethics: A Reader,* ed. Lois K. Daly (Louisville: Westminster John Knox, 1994), 52.
8. Sallie McFague, *The Body of God: An Ecological Theology* (Minneapolis: Fortress Press, 1993).
9. Mary Potter Engel, "Evil, Sin, and Violation of the Vulnerable," in *Lift Every Voice: Constructing Christian Theologies from the Underside,* ed. Susan Brooks Thistlewaite and Mary Potter Engel (San Francisco: Harper San Francisco, 1990), 155.
10. Jones, *Feminist Theory and Christian Theology,* 96.

A further critical development has been the recasting of sin into broader relational models that include a more fluid understanding of subjectivity. For instance, Thandeka has argued that the self constructed in terms of nineteenth-century paradigms fails to affirm the intersubjectivity of embodiment and relegates bodily epistemology to sin and fallen flesh.[11] When humanity understands itself as embodied and relational, women are provided with "a set of conceptual tools needed to understand right relationship as an interactive and inclusive embrace of irreconcilable differences."[12] Sin is therefore recast in terms of process, as a *becoming* within the complex web of relational identity. This can be seen in the brokenness of human existence (as opposed to sin) described by Catherine Keller,[13] or in accounts that seek to shift the theological landscape while abandoning individuals' sin for tragic accounts of original cosmic flaws.[14] Feminist rearticulations of sin, along with all self-consciously contextual theologies,[15] have offered a counternarrative of the "human condition" found in traditional accounts of sin. As a doctrine that wields great power, the feminist critique of typically masculine accounts of fallen humanity has been

---

11. Thandeka, "The Self between Feminist Theory and Theology," in *Horizons in Feminist Theology: Identity, Tradition, and Norms*, ed. Rebecca S. Chopp and Sheila Greeve Delaney (Minneapolis: Fortress Press, 1997), 80.

12. Ibid., 98.

13. Catherine Keller, *From a Broken Web: Sexism, Separation and the Self* (Boston: Beacon, 1986).

14. For instance, Kathleen M. Sands pushes toward interpretations of sin based on the tragic, critiquing the history of rationalism and dualism to argue for a concept of the conflicted tragic. She describes reality as the place where 'we must create what right and reason we can'." See Kathleen M. Sands, *Escape from Paradise: Evil and Tragedy in Feminist Theology* (Minneapolis: Fortress Press, 1994), xi.

15. Derek R. Nelson's survey of twentieth-century perspectives on sin is an excellent introduction to the developments in a number of contextual approaches to sin. See Nelson, *What's Wrong with Sin*. Of course, all theology is by its nature "contextual'." As feminist and other marginalized scholars have noted, the problem in employing language of contextual and systematic theologies (over and against each other) is that it allows dominant systematic approaches to ignore context and remain unnamed in regard to contexts of power.

a welcome relief for women seeking to live with grace and flourishing.[16]

In the process of constructing gendered accounts of sin, the historical underpinning of the doctrine of original sin is critiqued and deconstructed. No figure looms larger in this critique than Augustine, not only for his descriptions of active sin, but especially for his influential account of original sin.[17] It is not true, as is often alleged, that Augustine simply invented the doctrine of original sin. In a now-notorious essay on "The Politics of Paradise," Elaine Pagels gives the impression that Augustine diverges from tradition and creates original sin to further his political aims. She writes,

> The work from Augustine's later years, radically breaking with many of his predecessors, effectively transformed the teaching of the Christian faith. Instead of the freedom of the will and humanity's original royal dignity, Augustine emphasizes the bondage of the will by depicting humanity as sick, suffering, and helpless, irreparably damaged by the Fall. For that "original sin," Augustine insists, involved nothing else than Adam's prideful attempt to establish his own autonomous self-government. Astonishingly, Augustine's radical view prevailed, eclipsing for future generations of Western Christians the consensus of the first three centuries of Christian tradition.[18]

Many years later, Hans Küng argued that partly due to Augustine's Latin theology, Christian teaching after the fifth century succeeded the "Jewish-Christian paradigm and the Hellenistic paradigm of the

16. Rebecca Chopp navigates the tension between grace and sin in women's lives in Rebecca Chopp, "Anointed to Preach: Speaking of Sin in the Midst of Grace," in *The Portion of the Poor: Good News to the Poor in the Wesleyan Tradition*, ed. M. Douglas Meeks (Nashville: Abingdon, 1994).

17. Judith Chelius Stark writes, "Apart from Aristotle (whose writings on women are fairly limited), it is difficult to find a figure in Western thought whose legacy is more contentious and problematic in the views of many feminists than Augustine's'." See Judith Chelius Stark, "Introduction," in *Feminist Interpretations of Augustine*, ed. Judith Chelius Stark, Re-Reading the Canon (Pennsylvania: The Pennsylvania State University Press, 2007), 21.

18. Elaine Pagels, "The Politics of Paradise: Augustine's Exegesis of Genesis 1–3 versus That of John Chrysostom," *Harvard Theological Review* 78 (1985): 68.

early church."[19] Küng contends that Augustine arrives at original sin purely through a suspect exegesis of Rom. 5:12. In contrast to Pagel's accusations against Augustine's exegesis of Genesis, Küng claims that it is in Romans 5 that Augustine finds the explanation "why every human being, even the tiny infant, is poisoned in body and soul."[20] There is no doubt that Augustine became the champion par excellence of the doctrine of original sin, and that his explanation of human origins have been influential in perpetuating destructive attitudes toward women. However, to suggest that Augustine invented the doctrine of original sin is misleading at best. Most recently, historian Paula Fredriksen has traced the development of the early Christian concept of sin, noting the various explanations of sin's inception. For instance, in Valentinus it is the disorienting "Error" found in the original "Pleroma" that led to sin.[21] For Justin, it is the moment of unreason that causes sin, so that "intellectual error proceeds moral error,"[22] and for Origen a concept of "double creation" allows the theologian to describe the *hamartia* of the first created beings as a reaction, a "cooling" toward God. These primeval beings, though not initially culpable due to their inherited tendency to change, departed from God by small incremental degrees: "Their variety of stopping points, in effect, mark of the precosmic fall of the soul, the first sin."[23] Though equally creative and radical, Augustine's late account of original sin—in reference to the historical Adam and Eve—was clearly not the first proposed explanation for sin's

---

19. Hans Küng, *Women in Christianity*, trans. John Bowden (New York: Continuum, 2001), 29.
20. Ibid., 30.
21. What may be surprising to modern reading about Valentinus's account is the manner in which he links the tree of knowledge in the garden of evil to Christ's salvific action and not to sin (that is, Valentinus argues that Christ is crucified by Error and the primary symbol is of the parallel of cross and Eden's tree). See Paula Fredriksen, *Sin: The Early History of an Idea* (Princeton: Princeton University Press, 2012), 70.
22. Ibid., 80.
23. Ibid., 105.

inception. In her book *Original Sin*, Thata Wiley comes to a similar conclusion, noting that "to Augustine credit is rightly given for sharpening the clerical doctrine, but he never started from scratch."[24] And yet Augustine does provide the pivotal account of original sin, cast as a biological determination descending to all humanity from Adam and Eve. "More than any other single figure, Augustine created the dominant Christian way of telling the story of evil, and in his *Confessions* that story is stamped in an enduringly andocentric form. Christian theology is still entangled in the consequences of [this]."[25] It is this particular formulation of original sin that is consistently challenged by feminist theologians.

In light of current theoretical concerns around gender, an obvious question is raised in regard to the way gender is constructed in Augustine's account of original sin.[26] It is well known that Augustine's anthropology was tested and refined in the various controversies played out with his opponents. Though this makes a definite account of Augustine's construction of gender rather difficult, it is the clearly defined parameters around man and woman in the image of God that prove to be his legacy in Western thought. In the *City of God*, Augustine, through a historicizing of Genesis 1–3, insisted on Adam and Eve's original differentiated physical/sexual reality as the result of divine creation.[27] Not only were male and female created to be essentially different, the female was created in a way that both presupposes and reveals her subordination to the man. Augustine happily designates the woman as *help*, a second creation fitting for man. "If the question is to be asked, though,

24. Thata Wiley, *Original Sin: Origins, Developments, and Contemporary Meanings* (Mahwah, NJ: Paulist, 2002), 56.
25. Sands, *Escape from Paradise*, 16.
26. For Thata Wiley, this is the supreme concern regarding original sin in current debate for feminist theologians. See Wiley, *Original Sin*, 153.
27. *City of God* 12.24.

for what purpose it was necessary for this help to be made, no more likely answer suggests itself than that it was for the sake of procreating children—in the same sort of way that the earth is a help to the seed, so that the plant may born of each of them."[28] Putting aside the debate about how women exhibit the *imago dei*,[29] Augustine provides here a highly rigid account of the gender binary tied to humanity's inception. What's more, the second sex is divinely ordained to subordination and service. In this regard, feminist critique of Augustine's later interpretation of Genesis has been a necessary task.

Related to this is the powerful impression Augustine gives regarding sexuality. Notwithstanding the countless interpretations of Augustine's personal experiences with sexuality[30] (and with deference to the warning against engaging in popular psychoanalysis[31]), feminist theologians have engaged deeply with Augustine's attitudes toward sexual relationships. Although Augustine conceded that sex in paradise was without sin, this possibility seems to be solely based on the absence of the "disease" of disordered sexuality in the primeval estate. He writes,

> Why should we not suppose that before the sin those two human beings were able to control and command their genital organs for the procreation of children in the same way as their other limbs, which the soul moves for all kinds of action without any trouble or any sort of prurient itch or pleasure. . . . Why would it seem incredible that [God]

28. Saint Augustine, *On Genesis: A Refutation of the Manichees, Unfinished Literal Commentary on Genesis, The Literal Meaning of Genesis,* trans. Edmund Hill and Matthew O'Connell, The Works of Saint Augustine: A Translation for the 21st Century, ed. John E. Rotelle, vol. 13 (New York: New City, 2002), 9.5.

29. Rosemary Radford Ruether provides a succinct survey of Augustine's involvement in the debates around this matter. See Ruether, "Augustine: Sexuality, Gender, and Women," in Stark, *Feminist Interpretations of Augustine.*

30. Perhaps one of the more convincing accounts is Margaret Miles's description of Augustine's sexual addiction found in Margaret Miles, *Desire and Delight: A New Reading of Augustine's Confessions* (Eugene, OR: Wipf & Stock, 1991).

31. Stark, "Introduction," 9.

made bodies for the first human beings of such a kind, that if they had not sinned and straightaway contracted a sort of disease[?][32]

Utilizing his theory of concupiscence, Augustine argued that lust, or grasping and snatching at one's desires present in sexual acts, was indeed a sign of sin, and that although marriage (directed toward reproduction) was not sinful in itself, preference was "unmistakably on the side of celibacy and consecrated virginity."[33] In further sullying sexual acts, Augustine's description of the transmission of original sin is forceful:

> For we were all in that one man since all of us were that one who fell into sin through the woman who was made from him before sin. We did not yet have individually created and apportioned shapes in which to live as individuals; what already existed was the seminal substance from which we were to be generated. Obviously, when this substance was debased though sin and shackled with the bond of death in just condemnation, no man would be born of man in any other condition.[34]

Besides classifying sexual desire as sin itself, and arguing for the supremacy of celibacy, Augustine's highly problematic explanation for sin's transmission ensures that conception is tarnished by the impurity of sex. Consequently, Augustine has been charged with responsibility for the suppression of sexuality in Western theology,[35] and this understanding of Augustine's influence has produced various counterresponses among secular thinkers to "rescue sex from the Christians."[36]

32. Augustine, *On Genesis*, 13:11.18.
33. Stark, "Introduction," 28.
34. *City of God*, 13.14.
35. Küng, *Women in Christianity*, 30.
36. Clayton Sullivan writes, "Theologians after Augustine mimic his thought. They reason as follows: 'Since Augustine said it, it must be true.'" This is an extremely uninformed claim about the history of theological discourse on sin; however, it does provide insight into the popular reading of Augustine's influence. See Clayton Sullivan, *Rescuing Sex from the Christians* (New York: Continuum, 2006), 12.

The logical implications regarding reproduction and contraception are extremely significant for women's lived experience. In Augustine's account of original sin, with the claims regarding sexual desire and seminal transmission, the Manichaen position on sex and reproduction is inverted. While the Manichees taught that though sex was permissible for lower ranking auditors, contraceptive measures should be taken to avoid the ongoing entrapment of light in the darkness of new bodies,[37] Augustine swung from this procontraceptive and antireproductive ethic to an anticontraceptive and proreproductive ethic. Augustine articulates his adjusted position in *The Morals of the Manichees* and *The Morals of the Catholic Church*, while still affirming God's original intention of marital sex in *The Good of Marriage*. For him, even within a heterosexual monogamous marriage, sex that was not directed toward reproduction could be deemed sinful.[38] Contraception was therefore forbidden as a sinful corruption of God's design. In the twentieth century, feminist campaigns for free access to contraception have highlighted the physical and psychological cost of this position, a position still defended today by the Catholic Church.[39] Further questions have been raised about the political undertow of this theology of contraception, especially with regard to the options available to women incurring unwanted pregnancies. As Radford Ruether notes, "The denials of reproductive agency to women is one of the perduring and most egregious forms of violence to women. . . . All these disastrous consequences for women, for children, for humanity in general and its relation to world resources are denied by insisting

37. See Elizabeth Clark, "Augustine on Marriage," in *Feminism and Theology*, ed. Janet Martin Soskice and Diana Lupton, Oxford Readings in Feminism (Oxford: Oxford University Press, 2003), 250.
38. *The Good of Marriage* 6.6.
39. An early publication that has proven especially influential is John T. Noonan, *Contraception: A History of Its Treatment by the Catholic Theologians and Canonists* (Cambridge, MA: Harvard University Press, 1966).

that such passive acceptance of pregnancy and childbearing is women's 'natural' fate and duty."[40]

It is not surprising that many feminist theologians now advocate complete abandonment of the doctrine of original sin. Joy Ann McDougall shows how this abandon is played out in typically liberal approaches, as exemplified by Daphne Hampson. The logical outcome of prior rejections of divine sovereignty is to reject the symbolic order contained in conceptions of original sin as incurably oppressive.[41] In current poststructuralist approaches, the social contingencies of the subject ensure that any fixed human subject is impossible. Thus concepts like Foucault's genealogy of power prove far more amenable as theoretical tools. Margaret D. Kamitsuka provides an erudite example of this approach.[42] Certainly there is a lot to appreciate in these approaches, especially for the way they destabilize categories like gender and sexuality that seem cemented in traditional accounts of original sin. However, these revisionist approaches often give scarce attention to the theological intention of the doctrine or original sin or to how this doctrine may inform a contemporary Christian feminist agenda. In what follows, I wish to revaluate Augustine's doctrine of original sin as it relates to a theologically gendered account of creaturely difference. Rather than focus on the well-known version of original sin found in Augustine's later work, I will focus on the relatively early portrayal of original sin found in the *Confessions*. Though this is hardly a novel approach to Augustine's work,[43] I will argue for a quite different standpoint from which to view original sin. Here I agree with Margit Ernst-

40. Rosemary Radford Ruether, "Religion, Reproduction and Violence against Women: Essays on Religion and Violence," in *Weep Not For Your Children*, ed. Lisa Isherwood and Rosemary Radford Ruether, Religion and Violence (London: Equinox, 2008), 24, 25.

41. Joy Ann McDougall, "Sin—No More? A Feminist Re-Visioning of a Christian Theology of Sin," *Anglican Theological Review* 88, no. 2 (2006): 221.

42. Margaret D. Kamitsuka, "Toward a Feminist and Postmodern and Postcolonial Interpretation of Sin," *Journal of Religion* 84, no. 2 (2004): 179–211.

Habib: "Though in our day Augustine has been made responsible for almost everything that went wrong in theology, especially in relation to his understanding of original sin, the time has come to explore how Augustine might actually be helpful for a liberating theology."[44]

Augustine's Confession and Universal Origins: Sin, Difference, and Grace

Ten years after his baptism, and only a few years after becoming bishop of Africa, Augustine wrote the *Confessions*. Back in Africa, and cut off from the many *spiritales* whom Augustine befriended in Italy, the significance of his African upbringing was not lost on the bishop. In his classic biography, Peter Brown concludes that "the *Confessions* is very much the book of a man who had come to regard his past as training for his present career."[45] Margaret Miles, however, suggests the opposite, that Augustine saw the benefit in sharing his confessions and yet "never seemed to recognize, and never acknowledged, that the way—the journey—painful, damaging, and destructive as it was to himself and other human beings around him, was nevertheless, for him, a process of coming to what he described as a highly satisfying and productive synthesis in his life."[46] What Augustine did recognize

43. For instance, in quite the opposite fashion James J. O'Donnell has sought a clearer picture of Augustine's later life from the under-studied letters. See James J. O'Donnell, "Augustine's Unconfessions," in *Augustine and Postmodernism: Confessions and Circumfession*, ed. John D. Caputo and Michael J. Scanlon (Bloomington: Indiana University Press, 2005), 212–21. From a feminist perspective, E. Ann Matter draw a picture of Augustine's view regarding women's nature also through an isolated view of his letters, revealing a more charitable reading of Augustine in this regard. See E. Ann Matter, "De cura feminarum: Augustine the Bishop, North African Women, and the Development of a Theology of Female Nature," in Stark, *Feminist Interpretations of Augustine*, and also Colin Davis, *After Poststructuralism: Reading, Stories, Theory* (London: Routledge, 2004).

44. Margit Ernst-Habib, "'Chosen by Grace': Reconsidering the Doctrine of Predestination," in *Feminist and Womanist Essays in Reformed Dogmatics*, ed. Amy Plantinga Pauw and Serene Jones, Columbia Series in Reformed Theology (Louisville: Westminster John Knox, 2006), 83.

45. Genevieve Lloyd, *The Man of Reason: "Male"' and "Female" in Western Philosophy* (London: Routledge, 1984), 162.

was the "dark undertow of life"[47] coupled with the joy in which he was now able to confess to God. He begins with,

> Great are you O Lord, and exceedingly worthy of praise, your power is immense, and your wisdom beyond reckoning. And so we humans, who are due part of your creation, long to praise you—we who carry our mortality about with us, carry the evidence of our sin and with it the proof that you thwart the proud. Yet these humans, due part of your creation as they are, still do long to praise you. You arouse us so that praising you may bring us joy, because you have made us and drawn us to yourself, and our heart is unquiet until it rests in you.[48]

As the first publication of its kind,[49] a monological autobiography, the *Confessions* would have seemed radical to the late Roman citizen. In today's secularized "singular confessing society" (Foucault) there is little shock in such confessiography.[50] Post-Freudian concerns encourage the ongoing psychoanalysis of Augustine and the many references to his "ego."[51] Yet Björn Krondorfer rightly notes that Augustine's concerns are theological and not primarily psychological:

> It is, after all, religion—[Augustine's] pious religious imaginary—that allows him to report on himself in intimate detail. . . . The imagined

46. Margaret Miles, *Rereading Historical Theology: Before, During, and After Augustine* (Eugene, OR: Cascade, 2008), 104.

47. Ibid.

48. Saint Augustine, *Confessions*, trans. Maria Boulding, The Works of Saint Augustine: A Translation for the 21st Century, ed. John E. Rotelle, (New York: New City, 1997), 1.1.1.

49. Peter Brown notes that although pagan philosophers in the second and third centuries had developed a kind of "religious autobiography," the literary form offered in the *Confessions* was dissimilar to any precedent. Peter Brown, *Augustine of Hippo: A Biography*. Rev. ed. (California: University of California Press, 2000), 159.

50. This is a term coined by Björn Krondorfer to describe the particular mode of self-examination in which men have "attempted to reveal themselves to themselves and others'." Lorraine Code, "Taking Subjectivity into Account," in *Feminist Epistemologies*, ed. Linda Alcoff and Elizabeth Potter, Thinking Gender (New York: Routledge, Chapman and Hall, 1993), 8.

51. Julie B. Miller has provided a recent and exceptional example of a feminist psychological critique of Augustine, in which she examines the way Augustine's construction of the Trinity is reflected in his sexuality (and vice versa) and offers an alternative reading of Augustine's relationship with Monica (in an way that is explicitly feminist and not classically Freudian). See Julie B. Miller, "To Remember Self, to Remember God: Augustine on Sexuality, Relationality, and the Trinity," in Stark, *Feminist Interpretations of Augustine*, 243–79..

dialogical You in Augustine's *Confessions* is always God. Augustine, so to speak, imagines seeing himself through the eyes of God, and with this perspective he begins to gain knowledge of himself.[52]

The interplay of *confessant* and *confessor* as a literary device allows Augustine to move from introspection to theological treatise. For Augustine, confession is both the bearing of one's sinful self and testimony of God's revealed truth. Secondly, the *Confessions* are first and foremost a prayer, and that makes this a highly unusual text, providing a window into both Augustine's life and his theological convictions. Given Augustine's prebaptismal life—and especially his nine years as Manichaen devotee—the sincerity of his conversion along with his rapid rise to the episcopate were causes for concern. The contemporary translator of the *Confessions* Maria Boulding argues that though the confessions are not polemical, the Manichees are in Augustine's sights.[53] Annemaré Kotzé has mounted a convincing argument that many of Augustine's writing strategies in the *Confessions* are "eminently suited to communicate with a Manichaean audience" and even designed to convince practicing Manichaens of their error.[54] Original sin in the *Confessions* must therefore be placed against the backdrop of Manichaen beliefs and practices.

Assuming a position of intellectual superiority, Manicheanism presented a syncretistic and what seemed ascetic version of Christianity. Maintaining a dualistic cosmology—the kingdom of light verse the kingdom of darkness—the Manichaen faith taught that Yahweh of the Jewish scripture was a malevolent demon and the patriarchs were dirty old men.[55] Manicheanism also taught that

---

52. Code, "Taking Subjectivity into Account," 16.
53. Maria Boulding, "Introduction," in *Confessions*, 10.
54. These claims follow an extensive analysis of *Confessions* 3.6.10 through 3.10.18. See Annamaré Kotzé, "The 'Anti-Manichaean' Passage in *Confessions* 3 and Its 'Manichaean Audience,'" *Vigiliae Christianae* 62 (2008): 187.

creaturely differences—most notably gender—were inherently, or rather essentially, evil. In a gnostic vein, the Manichees were rationally disgusted by sex, procreation, and the female body. The elect suffering were entrapped "in the material world of bodies and objects, yearning to breathe free of their prisons and reunite with their spiritual homeland."[56] So while sex was permitted for lower members (auditors or hearers, such as Augustine), it was interpreted in a dualistic fashion, an act the soul could detach from and objectively disdain. What became another significant factor in Augustine's refutation of Manichaenism was the theodicy of the Manichaen system. In claiming evil to be an alien source that inhabits the material world, the Manichees could avoid guilt in their "good soul." The mind can remain untarnished. Augustine would reflect on this in the *Confessions*:

> It still seemed to me that is was not us who sin, but some other nature within us that is responsible. My pride was gratified at being exculpated by this theory: when I had done something wrong it was pleasant to avoid having to confess that I had done it, a confession that would have given you a chance to heal this soul of mine that had sinned against you.[57]

In the *Confessions*, Augustine responds to the Manichaen teaching by addressing these questions regarding evil's origin and the goodness of creation. What previously seemed impossible—that the God of the Jewish bible and the fully embodied Jesus were indeed God—becomes suddenly clear in Augustine's conversion to the authority of Scripture: "But scripture tells us that those who seek the Lord will praise him, for as they seek they find him."[58] In book 3,

55. That is, mostly in relation to polygamous practices and the highly sexual active communities narrated in Hebrew Scripture. See Lloyd, *The Man of Reason*, 50.
56. Miles, *Rereading Historical Theology*, 86.
57. Augustine, *Confessions*, 5.10.18.
58. Ibid., 1.1.1.

Augustine mounts an "extended refutation of Manichean objections to the Old Testament, suggesting that the problems disappear when scripture is interpreted correctly,"[59] that is, allegorically. Woven into the narrative of his youth and conversion, Augustine counters the dualistic account of creation and evil and presents a picture of human existence far more attentive to the limits of human freedom than he was willing to acknowledge while a Manichee. Well before the memorable conversion scene (notably interrupted with an extended discussion of free will), Augustine recalls his situation: "For me too a scourge was waiting there, in the guise of a bodily illness that brought me to death's door loaded with all the sins I had committed against you, against myself and against other people, evil deeds many and grievous over and above the original sin than binds all of us who die in Adam."[60] To correspond with this personal account of sin, Augustine argues right throughout the *Confessions* for the dignity and original goodness of the creation, a point brought to something of a climax in the closing passages of the *Confessions*:

> I heard your answer, O Lord my God, and from this truth I sucked out a drop of sweetness. I understood why some people do not find your creatures pleasing; they hold that you were driven by necessity when you built such things as the heavens and the constellations, and that these had already been created somewhere else and by some other power. You, they say, merely assembled them, fitted and welded them together when you were laboriously constructing the ramparts of the world after vanquishing your enemies, to barricade them in and ensure they would never again rebel against you. . . . It is different for people who see creation through your Spirit, for you are seeing it through their eyes. Thus when people see that these things are good, you are seeing that they are good; whatever created things pleases them for your sake, it is you who are arousing their delight in these things; and anything that gives us joy through your Spirit gives you joy in us.[61]

59. Kotzé, "The 'Anti-Manichaean' Passage in *Confessions* 3," 196.
60. Augustine, *Confessions*, 5.9.16.
61. Ibid., 13.30.45 to 13.31.46.

Rejecting Manichaean dualism, Augustine argues that all creaturely and embodied differences are part of God's good ordering of creation. The later technical account of original sin, and the more radical claims regarding sin's transmission through concupiscence, is not found in the *Confessions*. What Augustine presents is a grammar of creation, fall, and grace. This account is focused on the positive eros of creaturely beauty—where all things point beyond themselves to the Creator—and is contrasted with fallen eros, in which the fallen self both consumes and condemns creation. In the *Confessions*, original sin is not about disgust with sex or the (female) body.[62] On this point, as James J. O'Donnell has argued, Augustine's conversion to celibacy was largely due to Ambrose's claims about the superiority of Christian philosophy and the importance of celibacy as a mark of such "new philosophers." At the time of the *Confessions*, Augustine rules out sexual relationships for himself not because he believes sexual pleasure is a vice in itself, but because he concludes with Ambrose that "continence as the pedestal of piety" will be necessary in his new career as a Christian philosopher. Original sin is his way of explaining the malfunctions in creation without conceding that there is any evil thing anywhere in God's gracious act of creation.[63] Consequently, in book 2, during extended descriptions of Augustine's pubescent sexual exploits (roaming the streets of Babylon and wallowing in its "filth," 2.3.8), Augustine can still declare that "these lowest goods hold delight for us indeed, but not so much delight as does my God, who made all things; for in him the just man finds delight, and for the upright souls he himself is joy."[64] In

---

62. See James J. O'Donnell, *Augustine: A New Biography* (New York: Harper Perennial 2006), 74–78.

63. As Mary T. Clark has argued, Augustine counters Manichaean teaching of emanation with *creatio ex nihilo*, a doctrine that came to him from Scripture (*Confessions* 12.7.7). See Mary T. Clark, *Augustine*, ed. Brian Davies, Outstanding Christian Thinkers (Continuum: New York, 1994), 35.

64. Augustine, *Confessions*, 2.5.10.

book 5 he adds, "If sensuous beauty delights you, praise God for the beauty of corporeal things, and channel the love you feel for them on to their Maker."[65] As a theological device, original sin is about securing the essential *goodness* of all created things, especially the body and the delight embodied experience brings. Certainly Augustine would later develop problematic accounts of gender and sexuality, and yet the *Confessions* presents original sin in a way that demonstrates the positive function of this doctrine in a Christian grammar of creaturely goods. Notwithstanding his later tendencies toward sexual negativism, the Augustine of the *Confessions* has been "fully intellectually converted to the view of the body and the material world as good in their proper places."[66]

Augustine's Original Sin and Creaturely Difference: Some Correctives

From the picture of original sin that emerges in the *Confessions* there are significant possibilities opened up for Christian feminist discourse.

First, it has become clear that Christian scholarship needs to remythologize[67] the Genesis fall narrative. In *Remythologizing Theology* Kevin Vanhoozer tries to show the significance of scriptural mythos (mythos being "all the ways in which diverse forms of biblical literature represent and render the divine drama"[68]), and calls for a "spring back into metaphysics."[69] That Augustine would in some

65. Ibid., 5.12.18.

66. Sands, *Escape from Paradise,.*

67. This is a play off the work of Kevin J. Vanhoozer. Vanhoozer's claim to "remythologize" is in reference to "mythos," Aristotle's term for dramatic script. Thus the God who acts and speaks in and through the Bible is the basis of "first theology," the antithesis of Bultmann's "mythologizing." See Kevin J. Vanhoozer, *Remythologizing Theology: Divine Action, Passion, and Authorship*, Cambridge Studies in Christian Doctrine, ed. Daniel W. Hardy (Cambridge: Cambridge University Press, 2010).

68. Ibid., 7.

69. Ibid., 28.

works historicize Adam and Eve and the Genesis fall account is crucial for nearly every feminist critique of original sin. For Augustine, the historicizing of Adam was certainly bound up with his movement away from purely Platonic ideas of the soul toward a positive appreciation of incarnation of history.[70] But in a text so affirming of the created order and embodied experience as the *Confessions*, the lack of any literal Eve and Adam is striking. If *Confessions* can, without any such literalism, coherently affirm universal and personal sin coupled with the original goodness of creation, then I suggest it is equally possible to ignore the literalism Augustine later brings to the biblical creation and fall narratives. Certainly Augustine's own varied interpretations demonstrate the multiplicity of ways in which Genesis may be read. David Kelsey adopts the kind of "remythologizing" approach that I have in mind here. In his *Eccentric Existence*, Kelsey argues that theology must abandon genealogical accounts of original sin and reconstruct the doctrine in ways that are compatible with contemporary accounts of human origins. In Kelsey's comprehensive reconstruction, original sin is still cast as a universal bondage that demands personal responsibility and repentance, and yet its genesis is not claimed to be biological but rather social.[71] In remythologizing the Genesis creation and fall narratives, theological accounts of creation and sin are unburdened not only of the obvious scientific difficulties of Augustine's later claims regarding human creation and sin's transmission, but also unburdened of the enormously problematic implications of this heteronormative narrative.[72] As Margaret Kamitisuka notes, even feminist appeals to the Genesis account of

---

70. See Fredriksen, *Sin*, 113, 114.

71. David Kelsey, *Eccentric Existence: A Theological Anthropology*, 2 vols. (Louisville: Westminster John Knox, 2009), 430.

72. Of course, it is worth noting that this seems far removed from Vanhoozer's own intentions, even though I believe his "remythologizing" approach is valuable for a feminist project.

creation tend toward essentializing the gender binary and heteronormativity of the narrative. Remythologizing allows theological anthropology to imagine alternative meanings in the text: "Freeing this Genesis-based notion from any assumption about natural male/female binarism will disassociate the appeal to creation in the image of God from the unwanted entailment of a privileged compulsory heterosexuality."[73] Of course, Augustine has nothing like this in mind when writing the *Confessions*, but he does present a coherent account of original sin that does not rely on a literal reading of Genesis.

Second, a defense of original sin requires a clearer conception of how universalizing works in the discourse of this doctrine. There is no doubt that Augustine sought to universalize his personal story, which is at times obviously problematic. When recounting his concern regarding nocturnal emissions (occurring after his commitment to continence) Augustine turns easily toward theological conclusions,[74] a "rhetorical operation that is possible only because he presumes the male body normative."[75] Augustine is rightly interrogated for this rhetoric;[76] however, this does not necessarily prove that the universalizing impulse in theology is inevitably bad. Indeed, the universal gestures in the *Confessions* are generally not directed toward anthropological claims. Augustine is not seeking to say something isolated about the human condition, or even his own condition; his concern is to speak of the human condition in the presence of God. The universal claims Augustine makes in relation to original sin are claims about the status of creatures before

73. Kamitsuka, "Toward a Feminist and Postmodern and Postcolonial Interpretation of Sin," 209.
74. Augustine, *Confessions*, 10.30.41.
75. Code, "Taking Subjectivity into Account," 84.
76. Margret Miles offers a brief but illuminating insight into the way Augustine's sexuality helped him understand time and existence. See Margaret Miles, *Augustine and the Fundamentalist's Daughter* (Eugene, OR: Cascade, 2011), 186–88.

God. Just as Augustine interprets texts allegorically to push toward theological truths, so he tells the story of his own life to reveal something about God's creation. This does not excuse Augustine for assuming himself to be the normative expression of humanity, or for the essentializing claims he makes about women. However, it is to acknowledge that the universalizing of experience is not the problem per se. As Judith Butler argues, the problem with universalizing is not with universality, "but with an operation of universality that fails to be responsive to cultural particularity and fails to undergo a reformulation of itself in response to the social and cultural conditions it includes within its scope of applicability."[77] Remythologizing the Genesis creation and fall narratives is precisely a means by which such reformulation may take place. Discourse concerning original sin becomes problematic—with regard to the social and cultural conditions of creaturely difference—whenever it tries to move beyond universal claims about creation and fall to definitions of the root of sin or of the primary sin that holds all other sins together. These attempts nearly always flatten difference.[78] There is a long history of reading Augustine's description of desire in the *Confessions* as an explanation of the root of sin. Certainly desire is of paramount importance to Augustine, a means by which he is able to describe the right (and misguided) direction of our deepest yearning. However, desire does not function as a condition of sin in any absolute sense. As Julie B. Miller argues, the closest Augustine gets to claiming such a position refers to the "spontaneous falling away" of the will to love God above oneself. The human condition is therefore a loss

---

77. Judith Butler, *Giving an Account of Oneself* (New York: Fordham University Press, 2005), 6.

78. Therefore we might say humanity's totalizing desire to overcome difference and to homogenize toward sameness is at the interior of sin's complicated web. Seen in this perspective, sin says something (as Susan Thistlethwaite suggests) about the "depth of human intolerance of difference." See Susan Thistlethwaite, *Sex, Race and God: Christian Feminism in Black and White* (New York: Crossroad, 1989), 59.

of knowledge for God and oneself, a state more closely aligned to nihilism.[79] For many scholars, pride has served as the primary sin. Reinhold Niebuhr's account was the impetus for Valerie Saving's famous response that pride is a typically masculine and privileged means by which to view sin. Indeed many have responded by redefining the root of sin as a diffusion of the self, or betrayal of trust, or lack of self-care. And yet, Mary Potter Engel has shown how each of these approaches can be profoundly oppressive once one considers the myriad of contexts in which sin is perpetrated and experienced. Though we need all this language to speak adequately of our experience, it is simply not true or useful "to reduce sin to a single root metaphor."[80] Serene Jones comes close to this position, acknowledging the diversity of women's lives and their oppressions, and yet finally concludes that there is need for a "root metaphor for sin to hold these differences together."[81] No justification is given for this conclusion, and I suggest, following Engel, that a more accommodating metaphor for sin is that of "the hydra, a mythical monster that grew two new heads for every one that Hercules severed."[82] Further, it seems that original sin *is* the root metaphor, a universal doctrinal claim that names the proliferation of sin—individual, social, structural, relational, and all the ways in which we have come to understand how sin injures creation. If discourse concerning original sin can resist the temptation to introduce totalizing categories, then the cultural particularities of creaturely difference are not threatened by the universal scope of the doctrine; indeed the doctrine points to difference.[83]

79. Miller, "To Remember Self, to Remember God," 251.
80. Engel, "Evil, Sin, and Violation of the Vulnerable," 164.
81. Jones, *Feminist and Christian theology*, 112.
82. Engel, "Evil, Sin, and Violation of the Vulnerable."
83. It seems that David Kelsey presents something like this (refusing to name any other root metaphor than original sin itself) in *Eccentric Existence*. Kelsey uses three lenses to view sin, but does not tie them together neatly in a way that may provide new totalizing statements.

Original sin, seen in this light—an account that remythologizes the Genesis creation and fall narratives, and functions as a nontotalizing universal—will not only be viable for feminist theology, but will also play a vital role in securing the grammar of creaturely difference and dignity. Original sin is first and foremost a defense of the goodness of creation and therefore of all creaturely difference. Margret Miles argues that Augustine, in book 12 of the *Confessions*, is exercising a method of remembering and regathering a vision of God's good creation; and then in book 13 Augustine's interest shifts to questioning how God's good creation comes to be experienced so painfully and ambiguously. Original sin allows Augustine to hold these two things together.[84] The doctrine allows him to respond to the presence of evil while maintaining reverence for God's good creation. It both credits God for creaturely difference and explains something of humanity's inability to live with difference. Moreover, while purely structural or relational accounts often fail to provide an adequate response to the relation of victim and perpetrator and the pervasiveness of sin,[85] original sin becomes a means by which the sins against difference (e.g., sexism, racism, homophobia, and ableism) can be named in universal and catastrophic terms. Scholarship concerned with sin can demand attention to these matters while simultaneously providing a positive account of the goodness of created difference.

In addition, original sin brings fragmented humanity together theologically. Today theological attention to difference, subjectivity, and the multiplicity of contextual forces will demand a great deal

---

84. Miles, *Desire and Delight*, 112–15.

85. With regard the rhetoric of victim and perpetrator, Miroslav Volf has shown, through recounting his experience of life in war-torn Croatia, that boundaries around victim and perpetrator are ideologically drawn and that such rhetoric is nearly always driven by problematic factors. See Miroslav Volf, *Exclusion and Embrace: A Theological Exploration of Identity, Otherness, and Reconciliation* (Nashville: Abingdon, 1996).

of complexity and flexibility in anthropology. But it will not be adequate simply to translate discourse about sin into a totally immanent social critique. Joy Ann McDougall questions, for instance, if feminist theological approaches to sin have been seized by a pragmatic atheism.[86] One finds the reverse tendency in contemporary accounts of sin or evil that hypostatize sin into something "out there" but not located anywhere in particular; this is characteristic, for example, of tragic accounts of creation. When attention is not given to the theological dimension of sin talk we may become "unable to differentiate between created human goodness and actual sinful human life."[87] Christian theology needs to provide a coherent account of how sin relates to all humanity in light of the Christian narrative and where God stands in relation to fallenness. Original sin provides a unique way to meet these challenges and to bring fragmented humanity into a single framework without recourse to essentializing universals, and without discounting the continuing need for diverse approaches to specific relations and contexts.

Finally, original sin is ultimately a grammar of grace and life in God. In book 2 of the *Confessions*—after revealing his sexual exploits and thievery—Augustine declares, "How can I repay the Lord for my ability to recall these things without fear? Let me love you, Lord, and give thanks to you and confess to your name, because you have forgiven my grave sins and wicked deeds. By your sheer grace and mercy you melted my sins away like ice."[88] It is only the experience of God's forgiving grace that brings light to Augustine's sins; it is the universal availability of grace that brings light to the universal human condition. In recounting Calvin's conception of grace, Serene Jones

86. McDougall, "Sin—No More?," 219.
87. Nelson, *What's Wrong with Sin*, 185.
88. Augustine, *Confessions*, 2.7.15.

shows that for Calvin, "the doctrine of sin depends on a prior doctrine of grace."[89] It may be described as a grammatical rule of doctrine that sin talk is always essentially grace talk. Further, discourse regarding the origins of sin is always to be framed in reference to discourse of eschatological redemption. Without reference to the Christian eschatological narrative, theology forfeits its "unique explanatory power."[90] Precisely because the rhetoric of original sin is in fact a grammar of divine grace, the doctrine of original sin is primarily part of a grammar of talk about God, and it therefore nurtures thanksgiving, praise, and life surrendered to the presence of the Triune God.

Restless Hearts:
Prayer, the Presence of God, and Sin Interrupted

The *Confessions* are prayer from beginning to end. Each book is punctuated with psalm-like prayers and short cries of praise and adoration to the God of grace whom Augustine so dramatically encountered. Just as Isaiah bows down and cries, "Woe is me, . . . for my eyes have seen the King, the Lord of hosts,"[91] Augustine confesses both his sin and the presence of God's glory. In fact, in book 10 of the *Confessions*, Augustine makes it startlingly clear that his radical introspection and public confession have not yet made him fully aware of or present to himself: "For there is a dangerous infection here, and how far I am clear of it is not easy for me to discern. I am solely afraid about my hidden sins, which are plain to your eyes but not to mine."[92] His inner world has functioned throughout

89. Jones, *Feminist Theory and Christian theology*, 98.
90. McDougall, "Sin—No More?," 220.
91. Isa. 6:5 RSV.
92. Augustine, *Confessions*, 10.37.60.

the *Confessions* not primarily as a mode of self-discovery but as a means by which memory could lead him back to the knowledge and presence of God.[93] "That is why you have dwelt in my memory" writes Augustine, "and it is there I find you when I remember and delight in you."[94] The journey is clear; the dialogical relationship between sin and grace has led to life with God. Inasmuch as original sin points toward grace, grace points not only to the forgiveness of sin, but to life within the freedom and fullness of the Triune God.

Feminist theology has rightly interrogated the nature of confessional practices, and attention to dynamics of power in liturgical practices has been fruitful. Yet a confession of the kind Augustine envisages is neither negative nor oppressive. The realization of sin comes with the realization that one is in the presence of God. Indeed, just as "all have sinned," all too stand in the presence of God, all are invited into the grace-filled and transformative life that Augustine describes. In God's presence, sin is cut off by the interjection of God's free word of forgiveness. Just as sin reveals its ubiquitous power, God's word is present to all. Maria Boulding concludes her comments on the nature of Augustine's confession with this:

> In the closing books, and especially the last, Augustine ponders the mystery of God's creative Word which calls all creatures into being. . . . The word of confession is . . . not simply a statement of what is, of the present truth of oneself, seen and admitted in the light of God's presence, with all the liberation that implies. It is more than a static recognition; it is a creative process. The human speaker is at one with God who is creating him; he becomes co-creator of himself, constituting himself in being by confession. Words, as Augustine observed, are essentially signs; and they reach their fullest meaning as servants of self-transcendence.[95]

93. See Lloyd, *The Man of Reason*, 178. Of course, memory is problematic for Augustine, and there are times when memory of sin causes great anxiety, such as night times, when these memories return with particularly intense power. See Miles, *Desire and Delight*, 105.

94. Augustine, *Confessions*, 10.24.35.

For Augustine, the *Confessions* are born not simply out of redemption from a lapsed moral state, but are the discovery of all creatures' redemption and invitation into the Triune life.[96] We are left with the kind of prayer that reaches beyond itself, its own word, its articulation of personal desire. Augustine practices the prayer of confession primarily as a resting in the presence of the Triune God. It is as this prayer ensues that sin is found to be gloriously interrupted.

95. Boulding, "Introduction," 25.
96. Krondorfer draws a parallel between Augustine's new birth and the birth of the *Confessions* as the result of this union. Code, "Taking Subjectivity into Account," 95.

5

The Power of Sin and Epistemic Transformation

The hydra seems an apt metaphor for sin: a beast with many heads, so poisonous even its tracks are lethal. Sin is hard to define. It is naïve and dangerous to imagine sin with clear boundaries. And yet, in the sins we narrate against creaturely difference, there seems an inextricable relationship between sin and power. Perhaps no concept has received greater attention in postmodern discourse than that of power, and here no figure has loomed larger than Michel Foucault. Attending to the power *epistémè* of modernity has enabled those concerned with difference and oppression—especially feminists—to face the full force of totalizing and normalizing discourses. However, theologically this has created problems for traditional language of divine power, and the relation between God's power and power discourses has become unclear. In this chapter, I wish to show that while Foucault's insights into power relations are penetrating, Christian theology needs to offer a counternarrative to the practices of the self prescribed by Foucault. The art of living for Christians is not primary a work exercised upon the self. Instead, the Christian tradition points to the bodily and epistemic transformation of selves through prayer and encounter with divine power—a power that is quite different from anything captured by Foucault's analysis of power relations.

Michel Foucault and the Limits of Power

It is perhaps time to ask a whole new set of questions about the politics of reading Foucault. How can we, for example, read his texts outside the disciplinary regimes that have so far appropriated his work? How can we let his writing find a voice, a texture and complexity outside the packaged and predictable interpretations of previous readings? How can we release him from the chains of commodified knowledges which highlight, reify and stereotype the complex folds of a thinker? How can we take his work out of the reductive introductions, the shortsighted dismissals, the obscure categories, the normalising labels and the rash generalisations? How can we begin to make his work as complex as the life of the man?[1]

Against Christian, Jeremy Carette's challenge is clear: "I maintain that Foucault was an atheist and that his work on religion does not sustain a traditional theological worldview."[2] Such caution is wise; Foucault himself insisted that theology should remain separate from postmodern theory, and he criticized Derrida for what he believed was an unconscious theology evident in Derrida's work.[3] And yet Foucault has been widely appropriated in both Christian theology as well as broader feminist, queer, and cultural theories. Indeed, Foucault's work is now a major strand of "postmodern theology,"[4]

1. Jeremy R. Carrette, *Foucault and Religion: Spiritual Corporality and Political Spirituality* (New York: Routledge, 2000), ix.
2. Ibid., xi.
3. Brian Ingraffa, *Postmodern Theory and Biblical Theology* (Cambridge: Cambridge University Press, 1995), 6.

and it continues to challenge and stimulate thinking in areas such as Christian history, understandings of the self, human sexuality, and religious practices and belief. For feminists, the influence of Foucault's work has been felt most forcefully in the areas of knowledge and power.[5] Feminist scholarship continually returns to Foucault as a means of framing the complex relationships of knowledge, power, history, and context.

In *The Order of Things*, Foucault laid out the epistemological framework from which he would later develop as his interest diverged toward theories of power and subjectivity:

> The present study is an attempt to analyse this experience [of knowledge]. I am concerned to show its developments. . . . Language as it has been spoken, creatures as they have been conceived and grouped together, and exchanges as they have been practiced; in what way, then, our culture has made manifest the existence of order, and how, to the modalities of that order, the exchanges owed their laws, the living beings their constants, the words their sequence and their representative value, what modalities of order have been recognized, posited, linked with space and time, in order to create the positive basis of knowledge as we find it in employed in grammar and philology, in natural history and biology, in the study of wealth and political economy.[6]

In seeking out this "inner law" (definitions that expose resemblances and differences necessary for "order") Foucault was able to argue for the contingency of historical sciences along with the provisional character of any given epoch's *epistémè*. Foucault demonstrated this through his archaeology of not only philosophical research, but also

---

4. A description made in James Bernauer and Jeremy Carrette, "Introduction: The Enduring Problem: Foucault, Theology and Culture," in *Michel Foucault and Theology: The Politics of Religious Experience*, ed. James Bernauer and Jeremy Carrette (Aldershot: Ashgate, 2004), 1.

5. See Monique Deveaux, "Feminism and Empowerment: A Critical Reading of Foucault," in *Feminist Interpretations of Michel Foucault*, ed. Susan J. Hekman, Re-Reading the Canon (University Park, PA: Pennsylvania University Press, 1996), 211.

6. Michael Foucault, *The Order of Things: An Archaeology of the Human Sciences*, a translation of *Les Mots et le choses* (New York: Vintage, 1994), xxi.

of institutions, commercial practices, and everyday opinions. Later Foucault would remark of his approach, "I have tried to make, obviously in a rather particular style, the history not of thought in general but of all that 'contains thought' in culture, of all in which there is thought."[7] As he developed his work, the category of *epistémè* was superseded by his use of *discourse* and *archive*, terms that provided Foucault with a more flexible account of nondiscursive influences, and responded to his critics who saw his work as mere theory, unable to address the "relation between knowledge and human practice."[8] After his pivotal inaugural lecture at Collège de France,[9] Foucault clarified his revised interest in the production of knowledge and the tangled web of knowledge and power. It is against the backdrop of societal systems that Foucault would explore the manufacture of discursive subjects and the prevalence of benevolent power. As Axel Honneth summarizes, "Society can thus be interpreted as a social system nourished through the twin dispositions of 'power' and 'desire' in which discourse, portrayed precisely as an omnipresent stream of linguistic events, is an object of strategic conflict."[10] Foucault would go on to expose the constant struggles between differing powers enacting their will to truth, and would explore the manner in which competing knowledges were contested and rejected. This leads to important conclusions about the way truth claims are used: "The problem does not consist in drawing the line between that in a discourse which falls under the category of scientificity or truth, and that which comes under some other category, but in seeing historically how effects of truth are produced

---

7. Foucault, "Interview with Raymond Bellours," in *Aesthetics, Method, and Epistemology*, ed. James D. Faubion, *Essential Works of Michel Foucault, 1954–1984* (London: Penguin, 1998).

8. Michael Drolet, "Introduction," in *The Postmodernism Reader: Foundational Texts*, ed. Michael Drolet (New York: Routledge, 2004), 20.

9. Given in 1970. The lecture was entitled *The Discourse on Language*.

10. Axel Honneth, *The Critique of Power: Reflective Stages in Critical Social Theory*, trans. Kenneth Baynes (Cambridge: The MIT Press, 1993), 151.

within discourses which in themselves are neither true nor false."[11] Foucault's analysis of power has not been without its critics. At the end of his comprehensive study of power in Foucault, Honneth, for example, argues that Foucault was mistaken to interpret societal organizations as power complexes operating in a totalitarian fashion.[12] Further, his theories of power have been judged inadequate to the complexities of late capitalism.[13] In a similar vein, Marxist feminists have been especially cautious about alliances with Foucault.[14]

However, Foucault has done more than anyone to open up a critical dialogue around the subtle interplay between power and benevolent control. The will to power—or the will to truth—in Foucault exposes not only the dominating forces of knowledge production, but also the way subjects are regulated and controlled. From within a theological framework, Foucault's critique of power helps to unmask some of the intricacies of sin in language, society, institutions, and subjects.

Moreover, because power plays such a significant role in the categorizing and subjection of *different* bodies, the work of Foucault has warranted careful attention from feminists. Several themes have emerged as special areas of interest. Foucault raises relentless questions about the creation of norms by which individuals are categorized "as either normal or pathological."[15] For Foucault, norms are produced precisely as a way of managing differences. The

11. Michael Foucault, *Power/Knowledge: Selected Interviews and Other Writings, 1972–1977*, ed. Colin Gordon, trans. Colin Gordon et al (New York: Pantheon, 1980), 118.
12. Honneth, *The Critique of Power*, 303.
13. Ibid., 202.
14. See for instance, Shahrzad Mojab, "Muslim Women and Western Feminists: The Debate on Particulars and Universals," *Monthly Review* 50, no. 7 (1988): 19–30.
15. Margaret A. McLaren, "Foucault and Feminism: Power, Resistance, Freedom," in *Feminism and the Final Foucault*, ed. Dianna Taylor and Karen Vintges (Urbana, IL: University of Illinois Press, 2004), 224.

production of norms must therefore be interrogated on the basis of their presumed truth and their role in the management of knowledge. Foucault maintained this position until his death in 1982, stating, "If we do not take up the history of the relationship between the subject and truth from the point of view of what I call, roughly, techniques, technologies, practices, et cetera, which have linked them together and established their norms, we will hardly understand what is involved in the human sciences."[16] Judith Butler has leaned heavily on Foucault's work regarding norms in her discussion of gender. She argues that the gender norm "is a form of social power that produces the intelligible fields of subjects, and an apparatus by which the gender binary is instituted."[17] Hence Foucault's compendious studies of sexual norms (as well as the correction and punishment of the sexually abnormal[18]) has become integral to contemporary gender theory. Contained in this theory of norms is a peculiar "double bind"[19] in relation to human subjects. In what is often described as a negative (that is, one that refuses cataphatic statements) concept of the individual, Foucault's matrix of power/knowledge and normativity

---

16. Michael Foucault, *The Hermeneutics of the Subject: Lectures at the Collège De France 1981–1982*, ed. Frédéric Gros (New York: Picador, 2001), 188.

17. Butler, *Gender Trouble: Feminism and the Subversion of Identity*, 2nd ed. (New York: Routledge, 2008), 48.

18. Foucault laid the foundations of the normalizing practices of discourse on sexuality with the inception of categories of *deviant* and *pervert* in Michel Foucault, *The Will to Knowledge*, trans. Robert Hurley, vol. 1, *The History of Sexuality* (New York: Penguin, 1981). Notably, Foucault's challenge to modern "moral" Christian conceptions of sex, women, and erotica has been particularly unsettling. He notes, "The nature of the sexual act, monogamous fidelity, homosexual relations, chastity—it would seem that men of ancient times were rather indifferent, and that none of this claimed much of their attention or constituted very serious problems as far as they were concerned. But this picture is not accurate. . . . It thus seemed to me that a whole recentering was called for. Instead of looking for basic interdictions that were hidden or manifested in the demands of sexual austerity, it was necessary to locate the areas of experience and the forms in which sexual behaviour was problematized, becoming an object of concern, an element for reflection, and a material for stylization." Foucault, *The Use of Pleasure*, trans. Robert Hurley, vol. 2, *The History of Sexuality* (London: Penguin, 1992), 14–15 and 23–24.

19. A phrase used in Hubert Dreyfus and Paul Rabinow, *Michel Foucault: Beyond Structuralism and Hermeneutics*, 2nd ed. (Chicago: University of Chicago Press, 1983).

leads to an apparently ambivalent portrayal of the subjectivity. As John Caputo puts it, Foucault sees power as something that "produces individuals precisely in order to block individuality."[20] This does not entail the death or obliteration of the subject as is sometimes suggested,[21] but it points to a second theme of great significance to feminists, namely Foucault's concept of *discursive subjects*.

In light of Foucault's archaeological or genealogical approach to epistemology, his theory of discourse is always subject to historical specificities. Each epoch produces discourse that identifies and establishes the authority of knowledge claims. For Foucault, this meant problematizing the subject to an unsettling level, a move that required a revision of whatever might generally be meant by consciousness or subjectivity. He states,

> This historical contextualisation needed to be something more than simply the relativisation of the phenomenological subject. I don't believe that the problem can be solved by historicizing the subject as posited by the phenomenologists, fabricating a subject that evolves through the course of history. One has to dispense with the constituent subject, to get rid of the subject itself, that's to say, to arrive at an analysis that can account for the constitution of the subject within a historical framework. And this is what I would call genealogy, that is, a form of history which can account for the constitution of knowldeges, discourses, domains of objects etc., without having to make reference to a subject which is either transcendental in relation to the field of events or runs in its empty sameness throughout the course of history.[22]

20. John Caputo, "Madness, Hermeneutics and the Night of Truth," in Bernauer and Carrette, *Michel Foucault and Theology*, 128.
21. For instance, feminist Nancy Harstock has consistently claimed that Foucault discounts the possibility of subjectivity: "Rather than getting rid of subjectivity or notions of the subject as Foucault does and substituting his notion of the individual as an effect of power-relations, we need to engage in the historical, political, and theoretical process of constituting ourselves as subjects as well as objects of history. We need to recognise that we can be the makers of history as well as the object of those who have made history." See Nancy Hartsock, "Foucault on Power: A Theory for Women?," in *Feminism / Postmodernism*, ed. Linda J. Nicholson, Thinking Gender (New York: Routledge, 1990), 170, 171.
22. Foucault, *Power/Knowledge*, 117.

Thus, a discursive subjectivity in Foucault's account is "more than ways of thinking and producing meaning."[23] Discourse not only exercises power over the mind but also ultimately over the body in the subject produced. Further, the discursive production of subjects should not be confused with the effects of power; indeed, Foucault speaks of the subject as the "very material of power, the thing through which power finds its expression."[24] Though this is the area in which Foucault has been most criticized by feminists,[25] it is also an area where his influence is felt the most acutely. In the libertine or humanist models of subjectivity that feminists have often used in the past, it was easily imagined that a woman's "self" had somehow been lost. This is clear in the language of recovery and retrieval, of pulling women "back" into some foundational or original mode of subjectivity.[26] Though "woman" in Foucault's account is socially constructed in discursive practices, "she none the less exists as a thinking, feeling subject and social agent, capable of resistance and innovations produced out of the clash between contradictory subject positions and practices."[27] Precisely because subjects are able to reflect on the discursive elements of knowledge production, power—which is not necessarily bad, simply ubiquitous—is always connected to resistance. Foucault's analysis of the predicament of the discursive subject, combined with his longstanding work on the way power operates through forms of disciplinary practices and self-surveillance,

23. Chris Weedon, *Feminist Practice and Poststructuralist Theory*, 2nd ed. (Oxford: Blackwell, 1997), 105.
24. Nick Mansfield, *Subjectivity: Theories of the Self from Freud to Haraway* (New York: New York University Press, 2000).
25. For instance, Rosi Braidotti argues rather vehemently against Foucault's account of subjectivity in Rosi Braidotti, *Nomadic Subjects: Embodiment and Sexual Differences in Contemporary Feminist Theory* (New York: Columbia University Press, 1994), especially chapter 7.
26. Ladelle McWhorter critiques this element of dominant feminism and suggests the popular "subject" of such feminism silences creativity and ultimately leads to a defensive conservatism. See Ladelle McWhorter, "Practicing Practicing," in *Feminism and the Final Foucault*, ed. Dianna Taylor and Karen Vintges (Urbana, IL: University of Illinois Press, 2004), 152–56.
27. Weedon, *Feminist Practice and Poststructuralist Theory*, 121.

led him eventually to the critical theme of his later work: *practices of the self.*

Foucault was concerned to respond to claims of pessimistic nihilism in his earlier conceptions of power and the subject. His genealogical accounts fail to prescribe the kind of social remedies that liberationists had hoped for. However in turning to the study of ethical self-formation of ancient philosophical life, Foucault conceives a "counter attack" against modern systems of power.[28] Margaret A. McLaren offers a compelling argument in favor of Foucault's practices of the self, and suggests that it is only in reading the late Foucault that one can understand the political, nonnormalizing, and emancipatory character of practices of the self.[29] In his seminal address *Technologies of the Self,* Foucault gathered his thinking to date (rather loosely) around this theme:

> We must understand that there are four major types of "technologies," each a matrix of practical reason: (1) technologies of production, which permit us to produce, transform, or manipulate things; (2) technologies of signs systems, which permit us to use signs, meanings, symbols, or signification; (3) technologies of power, which determine the conduct of individuals and submit them to certain ends or domination, an objectivizing of the subject; (4) technologies of the self, which permit individuals to effect by their own means or with the help of others a certain number of operations on their own bodies and souls, thoughts, conduct, and way of being, so as to transform themselves.[30]

As a technology of potential resistance, "care of the self" in the ancient world was equally concerned with care of the city; the wider context of the ethical was the political. It was expected that care

---

28. Dianna Taylor and Karen Vintges, "Introduction: Engaging the Present," in Taylor and Vintges, *Feminism and the Final Foucault,* 3.
29. McLaren, "Foucault and Feminism."
30. Originally presented at the University of Vermont in the fall on 1982. Michel Foucault, "Technologies of the Self," in *Technologies of the Self: A Seminar with Michel Foucault,* ed. Luther H. Martin et al. (Cambridge, MA: University of Massachusetts Press, 1988), 18.

of one's one philosophical and ethical formation would be an act of care for the city. Not only do such practices include diet and exercise, but also writing, learning, and contemplation of oneself for purposes of purification.[31] Ultimately, Foucault looks here to the ancient practice of *askesis*; as *askesis* becomes ethos, it is, Foucault argues, "a process of becoming more subjective."[32] It is through such practices that power can be self-directed as an alternative work upon the body. This concept of practices of the self has become critical to contemporary feminist theory.[33] As a double-edged sword, Foucault's earlier concepts of power/knowledge not only provide insight into the operation of totalizing power, but also challenge the common remedial strategies of liberationist approaches.[34] As Sharon Welch comments, "How do we act after we accept Foucault's challenge and realise that there are no fool proof formulas, that all of our actions are . . . subject to error and challenge?"[35] In practices of the self, feminists find a way to imagine both resistance and transformation as a way of response to Foucault's devastating analysis of power. For Judith Butler,

> to intervene in the name of transformation means precisely to disrupt what has become settled knowledge and knowable reality, and to use, as it were, one's unreality to make an otherwise impossible or illegible claim. I think that when the unreal lays claim to reality, or enters its domain, something other than a simple assimilation into prevailing norms can and does take place. The norms themselves can become rattles, display their instability, and become open to resignification.[36]

31. Ibid., 33.
32. Ibid., 35.
33. For instance, *Feminism and the Final Foucault* is a book of fourteen essays entirely dedicated to the exploration of contemporary feminism and Foucault's ethos of self-care. See Taylor and Vintges, "Introduction: Engaging the Present."
34. See Bat-Ami Bar On, "Marginality and Epistemic Privelidge," in *Feminist Epistemologies*, ed. Linda Alcoff and Elizabeth Potter, Thinking Gender (New York: Routledge, 1993), 93–95.
35. Sharon Welch, "'Lush Life': Foucault's Analytics of Power and Jazz," in *The Blackwell Companion to Postmodern Theology*, ed. Graham Ward, Blackwell Companions to Religion (Oxford: Blackwell, 2003), 86.

Unitive Prayer and the Limits of Discourse

In Foucault's account of the practice of the self, subjective transformation is in one's own hands. To resist and offer a counterattack to totalizing powers, one must exercise the types of disciplines that produce alternatives discourse/s and subvert the self produced by dominant systems of control. However, Christian practices offer a counternarrative, where the self is "worked on" through bodily and epistemic transformation that comes from outside of oneself. This is not one of the many powers within a social system, but is the power of divine presence. As David Tool points out, Foucault offers a possibility of resistance, but it is only a contingent and provisional resistance; he cannot point to anything beyond the self that might fundamentally disrupt the rule of "principalities and powers."[37] Hence, while Foucault comes to affirm the possibility of "mysticism as revolt,"[38] he is ultimately unable to point toward the power of divine presence or the transfiguring meaning of Christian practices. At the same time, feminist attempts to consider power and empowerment have been stunted by extreme caution; efforts to exercise "power games" alert to every possibility of domination will tend to falter in the face of difference.[39] Interestingly, the renewed awareness in recent Christian scholarship in apophatic and mystical traditions has taken place in the context of sustained dialogue with poststructuralist writing. Though theologians engaging with such traditions have, as Martin Laird observes, tried to find a way to move beyond the closed "ontotheological fists" of postmodernism, they generally do not address "the practicalities of what must happen to

---

36. Judith Butler, *Undoing Gender* (New York: Routledge, 2004), 28.
37. David Toole, *Waiting for Godot in Sarajevo: Theological Reflections on Nihilism, Tragedy, and Apocalypse* (Boulder, CO: Westview, 1988), 269, 270.
38. For an insightful exposition of this theme, see Grace Jantzen, *Power, Gender, and Christian Mysticism* (Cambridge: Cambridge University Press, 1995).
39. Welch, "'Lush Life,'" 85.

the discursive cognitive strategizing of the one who would encounter this God beyond all discursive knowing."[40] Christian attempts to test the limits of discourse and of power/knowledge require greater attention to embodied Christian practice, a practice that is understood not so much as a species of religious experience but as a way of life.[41]

A common theme in premodern traditions of Christian prayer was the need to quieten discourse. Martin Laird suggests that for the fourth-century monk Evagrius, the discursive mind was the stumbling block to prayer, and prayer was the "letting go of concepts."[42] In the ancient world, discourse could be overcome, and it was possible to distinguish between discursive and nondiscursive states. Here prayer functioned as a means of transcending the normal practices of thinking, speaking, and hearing. Knowing God was assumed to involve something quite outside the normal bounds of what is normally called "knowing." Mary Jane Rubenstein makes a similar claim in relation to contemporary concerns with theological method and apophaticism. Commenting on the impasse between Derrida and Jean-Luc Marion, she suggests that ontological debate misses the point: "The error of ontotheology is not using the word 'Being' to refer to the deity, but deifying being as knowledge, and by extension, deifying the knowing subject itself." So for Rubenstein, the problem is with the objectifying epistemology behind such strategies. The self that knows God abandons all knowledge of both the self and the divine.[43]

40. Martin Laird, "The 'Open Country Whose Name is Prayer': Apophasis, Deconstruction, and Contemplative Practice," *Modern Theology* 21, no. 1 (2005): 141.

41. Martin Laird argues that a key problem in current trends toward apophaticism is the tendency to abstract the apophatic verse cataphatic element of theological discourse, and he reminds readers that the apophatic tradition cannot be reduced to a philosophical strategy. "It is a simple life that leads to the experience of silence . . . and not merely to an apophatic style of theological thinking and writing." Ibid.

42. Ibid., 151.

43. Mary-Jane Rubenstein, "Unknow Thyself: Apophaticism, Deconstruction, and Theology after Ontotheology," *Modern Theology* 19, no. 3 (July 2003): 393.

Sarah Coakley shows in a lengthy essay that the texts of women mystics (and their bodily responses in prayer) push the boundaries of epistemology and discourse. Ironically, Coakley's essay is concerned to show that these texts, and particularly the work of Teresa of Avila, do not quite work with the epistemic purposes contemporary philosophers have in mind.[44] Though affirming the use of what she calls epistemic "soft centres" (trust, credulity, and testimony) as bulwarks against scepticism in the postmodern context, Coakley argues that contemporary philosophers have failed to take seriously Teresa's rationality. Teresa speaks about the stages of ascent as movements away from discourse that ultimately end in the self being completely unified in its response and taken up "into God in a way that also temporarily suspends its bodily movement and its sensations."[45] Teresa describes this stage of prayer as something beyond the boundaries of discourse: "How this prayer they call union comes about and what it is, I don't know how to explain. . . . I wouldn't know the proper vocabulary."[46] In this, Coakley suggests, what contemporary philosophy often calls "reason" has gone well beyond its normal limits, into the "dark ineffable realm" of divine union.[47] Not only has discourse been silenced, but the bodily senses are also taken up into the divine life. Teresa witnesses to a self that is worked on in ways she can neither explain nor understand. And yet she "knows" that nothing will cause her peace in God to leave.[48] The

---

44. Coakley critiques Richard Swinburne, Reformed Epistemologies (Nicholas Wolterstoff and Alvin Plantinga), and William Alston for their stereotypical assumption of the feminine for justificatory purposes in analytic philosophy of religion. Sarah Coakley, "Contemporary Religious Epistemology: The Turn to 'Femininity,'" in *Analytic Theology: New Essays in the Philosophy of Religion*, ed. Oliver D. Crisp and Michael C. Rea (Oxford: Oxford University Press, 2009), 284–312.
45. Ibid., 296.
46. Teresa of Avila, *Life*. Cited in Coakley, "Contemporary Religious Epistemology," 297.
47. Coakley, "Contemporary Religious Epistemology," 300.
48. Teresa of Avila, *The Interior Castle: Study Edition*, ed. and trans. Kieran Kavanaugh and Otilo Rodriguez (Washington, DC: ICS), 437.

normal configurations of knowledge, truth, and power have been transformed and Teresa is no longer the same self—though she could not be said to have achieved this herself through any self-directed "technology."

Though the prayer of union was originally described by Teresa as occurring in sporadic encounters with the divine, by the time of writing *The Interior Castle* she could speak of a permanent union in which she experiences the tension of complete union with God at one level, and the ongoing trials and tribulations of embodied life at another. In her discursive transformation, Teresa is empowered to live her bodily existence as even her material concerns are brought into the presence of God. Thus Teresa is no longer talking about moments of religious experience, but what might be called an ontology of mystical union. Coakley writes, "Whatever this state of union is, it is surely this that . . . [philosophy] should be interested when it attempts to explicate the significance of 'mystical theology' for epistemology. Here we do not so much grasp or "perceive" God, but more truly God grasps us."[49] Teresa's union with God, brought about through contemplative practices, produces a subject both seeking and finding transformation. In Foucault's terms, the self might be said to be worked upon in ways that evade discursive control. In her study of Teresa, Coakley points to an experience beyond practice and language, opening on to a very different ethos from anything envisaged in Foucault's "care of the self." In her broader theological project, Coakley evokes silence as the core of the "contemplative matrix"[50] in which the relation between power, language, and bodies is radically remapped. In contemplation, Coakley argues, one may "meet the ambiguous forms of worldly

---

49. Coakley, "Contemporary Religious Epistemology," 300.
50. Coakley, *Powers and Submissions: Spirituality, Philosophy and Gender*, Challenges in Contemporary Theology (Oxford: Blackwell, 2002).

power in a new dimension, neither decrying them . . . nor being enslaved to them, but rather facing, embracing, resisting or deflecting them with discernment."[51]

If theologians work with the assumption that transformation happens at the Foucauldian level of discourse, then we will have to conclude that nothing gets through Foucault's net of power. But within Christian traditions of prayer and displacement, one finds transformative possibilities in which power and discourse are superseded through a divine power that transgresses—because it does not belong to—worldly webs of discourse or control.

The Triune life and Divine Power

Though I have been using the language of *power* in relation to God, such talk of divine power remains problematic for most feminist theologians. As Catherine Keller argues,

> Assumed omnipotence, despite (or perhaps because of) the variety of persuasive alternatives now available, continues to dominate Christian imagination. It holds us captive to the "bad faith" of a systemic self deception. To heal itself, theological power rhetoric requires a moral account of the character of this power and, therefore, of power itself—of the matrix of meanings we mean when we deploy power language.[52]

Keller's remarks betray the assumption that divine power is analogous to "power" as Foucault and other postmodern thinkers understand it. Lurking within the analogy is the assumption too that divine and worldly powers can only be related to one another by contrast and opposition.[53] In this way, divine power becomes no more than a

---

51. Coakley, "Prologue: Powers and Submissions," in *Powers and Submissions*, xix.
52. Catherine Keller, "Power Lines," *Theology Today* 52, no. 2 (1995): 188.
53. In *God and Power*, Keller claims "the idolatry of a 'divine' finite sovereignty is exceeded only by the divinisation of sovereignty itself. Historically, divine omnipotence was only achieved

projection of (and continuation of the problems with) human power. And Keller's response to this knot of theological misunderstanding is a wholesale abandonment of divine omnipotence in favor of simply a *different* power, which means we are ultimately consigned to the never-ceasing struggle of one (finite) power against another.[54]

The Christian doctrinal tradition does not speak of transcendence, of creative power, of the power of re-creation, as if these belonged to a larger list of "principalities and powers." Divine power is different and does not operate on the same level as Foucauldian discursive power. Talk of divine power requires a radicalized grammar with a severe caution about analogies. Theological language about power and sin does not simply spill over into the language of divine omnipotence. Talk of divine power is characterized by the way it makes space for the kind of transformation that one finds in contemplative traditions. In prayer, power does not dominate but creates space for the self, its body, and its future in God. In practices of prayer, women and men are invited to wait on the "presence of God." Here omnipotence is a resource that creates personal union—a union that includes (but is not confined to) the domain of discourse. What occurs in the encounter between human beings and divine power is not a struggle for dominance or control, but what Sarah Coakley calls a "willed effacement to a gentle omnipotence."[55] Here the self lovingly receives and is loving received by the Triune life of God.

---

as a mimicry of the empire'. Keller, *God and Power: Counter-Apocalyptic Journeys* (Minneapolis: Fortress Press, 2005), 51.

54. Keller, "Power Lines," 197.

55. Sarah Coakley, "Kenosis: Theological Meanings and Gender Connotations," in *The Work of Love*, ed. John Polkinghorne (Grand Rapids: Eerdmans, 2001), 34, 37.

PART III

Trinity

6

———

Gendered Economy

The Trinity and Subordination in Contemporary
Systematic Theology

Ultimately, the Christian doctrines of creation and fall find their grounding in the doctrine of God. This has been implicit in every part of my argument so far. The significance of the doctrines of creation and fall for considerations of difference lies in the way these doctrines describe the relation between creatures and the Triune God. In the final section of this book, I will explore the critical importance of the doctrine of the Trinity for the problems of difference.

Feminist theologians have been cautious of talk regarding the economic Trinity. Not only has the relationship of Father-Son-Spirit been used to argue for hierarchy and subordination, the feminization of the Spirit by some feminists has been seen as potentially reinforcing women's subordination. How can feminist theologians articulate the grammar of the doctrine of the Trinity in a manner that affirms human difference? In what follows I will be proposing the model of "Triune communicative acts" recently advocated by Kevin Vanhoozer as a means by which discourse about the economic Trinity may incorporate creaturely difference.

Rahner's rule[1] has proven an impetus for particular attention in modern theology to the God of history. It is clear that this emphasis is fruitful in feminist discourse.[2] However, feminist revision on the Trinity has often been too quick to leave behind the economic Trinity in the interests of speculation on the immanent Triune relations. Elizabeth Johnson, for example, argues that language about the salvific action of God intends to point via analogy toward the "Holy Mystery."[3] Johnson's account highlights one of the clear challenges for gendered notions of the economic Trinity. Just how far we take Rahner's rule will determine to what extent metaphysical claims are made about the revealed Triune God. One may argue that Rahner only ever intended to use his rule as an epistemological device, but metaphysical positions such as Robert Jenson's[4] have provided reason enough for concern among feminist theologians. Metaphysical revelation is not the only issue that makes gendered readings of the divine economy challenging. The ongoing debate about the *filioque* runs the risk of permanently entangling the

1. That is, "the economic Trinity is the immanent Trinity, and the immanent Trinity is the economic Trinity." See Karl Rahner, *The Trinity* (New York: Herder and Herder, 1970).

2. Stanley Grenz makes the interesting observation that even as a feminist not highly concerned with the parameters of the traditional doctrine, Catherine Keller finds the social analogy of the Trinity to have the potential to "undermine the conceptual essence of patriarchy." Keller, *From a Broken Web: Sexism, Separation and the Self* (Boston, Beacon, 1986), 167. Cited in Stanley J. Grenz, *The Social God and the Relational Self*, The Matrix of Christian Theology (Louisville: Westminster John Knox, 2001), 5.

3. Elizabeth A. Johnson, *She Who Is: The Mystery of God in Feminist Theological Discourse*, 10th anniversary ed. (New York: Crossroad, 1992), 200.

4. This position is most obvious in Jenson's essay, "The Father, He . . . ." Jenson argues that "father" language for God is neither trope nor metaphor but points to God's ontological status, an argument based on the Gospel accounts of Jesus' references to God as Father. Robert W. Jenson, "The Father, He . . . " in *Speaking the Christian God: The Holy Trinity and the Challenge of Feminism*, ed. Alvin F. Kimmel Jr. (Grand Rapids: Eerdmans, 1992), 95–119.

doctrine of the Trinity in a web of hierarchy and subordination. Psychological analogies may be employed to reduce the threat of subordinationism, but these often come at the expense of social and communal representations. In either instance, reference to biblical revelation proves an imposing obstacle, as it clearly develops themes of origin, procession, and dominion within the Trinity. Though history is the arena in which feminist readings seek emancipatory paradigms, it has not proven the most effective resource. In this chapter, I will first consider the contribution of three recent theologians, Catherine LaCugna, Leonardo Boff, and Gavin D'Costa, each of whom has tried to address some of the issues raised by feminists while working within frameworks of traditional doctrinal theology. By evaluating these attempts, I hope to highlight the ongoing challenges for feminist readings of the economic Trinity. In light of this evaluation, I will finally suggest an alternative framework—drawing on a recent proposal by Kevin Vanhoozer—in which we may find an understanding of the economic Trinity that is both theologically coherent and able to support a gendered reading.

LaCugna

Catherine LaCugna reiterates Rahner's concern to connect Trinitarian doctrine more closely to the world.[5] In rejecting Western (and at times Eastern[6]) foundations for Trinitarian theology, traditions that she argues have eclipsed the doctrine of the economic

---

5. Daniel J. Treier and David Lauber, *Trinitarian Theology for the Church* (Downers Grove, IL: InterVarsity, 2009), 8.
6. Grenz makes the observation that in this LaCugna differs from Zizoulous, for whom the Cappadocians emerge as unqualified heroes. Instead, LaCugna deems the Eastern fathers to be part of the problem. See Stanley J. Grenz, *Rediscovering the Triune God: The Trinity in Contemporary Theology* (Minneapolis: Fortress Press, 2004), 151.

Trinity,[7] LaCugna brings into question the validity of any discourse around the immanent Trinity. She writes,

> The immanent Trinity is not transhistorical, transempirical, or transeconomic. Nor is the immanent a "more real" God—more real because the mode of discourse used to describe it is ontological. Rather, to speak about God in immanent trinitarian terms is nothing more than to speak about God's life with us in the economy of Christ and the Spirit.[8]

In her historical evaluation, LaCugna cites the Western step of separating *theologia* from *oikonomia* as a critical error on the part of the church. Yet LaCugna was not satisfied simply to reinsert the economic Trinity back into Trinitarian discourse; her contribution was far more radical. In declaring that theology proper and soteriology are inextricably intertwined, LaCugna hopes to place the focus of all Trinitarian speculation firmly on the economy of redemption. The "immediate import" of Rahner's theology of God, according to LaCugna, is soteriological.[9] That her own construction is a development on Rahner is clear to LaCugna; she rephrases Rahner's rule to say, "Theology is inseparable from soteriology, and vice versa."[10]

Though this is not how Rahner's axiom is usually interpreted, it is one interpretation in which concepts of the immanent and economic Trinity are linked as "closely and inextricably as possible."[11] In practical terms, LaCugna speaks of the Trinity's function in elucidating the demands of the gospel, and helping us to understand how personal conversion is related to social transformation and what

---

7. Catherine Mowry LaCugna, *God For Us* (New York: Harper Collins, 1991), 70.
8. Ibid., 229.
9. Ibid., 211.
10. Ibid.
11. Roger E. Olson and Christopher A. Hall, *The Trinity*, Guides to Theology, ed. Sally Bruyneel et al. (Grand Rapids: Eerdmans, 2002), 109.

constitutes a right relationship in community.[12] Within this framework, LaCugna also builds on the notion of personhood as communion and points toward the salvation experience as our becoming "by grace what God is in nature."[13] With her emphasis on the realization of redemptive action in history, LaCugna's reading of the economic Trinity clearly resonates with concerns regarding full personhood and experience of the divine. And of special importance for feminists is LaCugna's deconstruction of monarchy in the Godhead. In evaluating the reign of the economic Trinity, LaCugna argues that the key lies in both Jesus Christ and in the "monarch" of such governance.[14] She suggests that the Greek fathers conceptualized monarchy in terms of persons[15] and not substance, and thus a communal reign was imagined, a *triadikē archē*. "If this trinitarian monotheism had prevailed, one can imagine that a different political and social order likewise would have prevailed."[16] She elaborates,

> The doctrine of the Trinity worked out by the Cappadocians dared the Christian imagination to relinquish all biological, cultural, political, and commonsense notions of fatherhood, in order to think of God correctly, according to the "true theology." The Cappadocians urged the church to think of God's fatherhood not as self-sufficiency or isolation or the inability to share self with another, but as relation to another who is equal.[17]

LaCugna's conception of the economic Trinity also allows her to address the pressing sociopolitical issues that have seen others move away from the doctrinal redemption narrative. But her work has

12. Catherine Mowry LaCugna, "The Practical Trinity," *Christian Century* 109, no. 22, (July 1992): 679.
13. LaCugna, *God For Us*, 1.
14. Ibid., 389.
15. This is largely because LaCugna, like Zizioulous, argues that the Cappadocians understood the "Father" as eternally the Father of the Son. Hence personhood becomes understood as community.
16. LaCugna, *God For Us*, 391.
17. Ibid., 393.

been criticized for modalistic overtones,[18] or for focusing on the Father at the expense of Son and Spirit in a way that has "more than a hint of subordinationism."[19] Ted Peters criticises LaCugna's bonding of divine life to the temporal,[20] and others have questioned whether LaCugna has done justice to the concept of divine freedom (an aspect that has critical implications for the doctrine of creation) in diminishing the ontological distinction between the immanent and economic Trinity.[21] For Grenz, instances when LaCugna hints toward the reality of God *in se* suggest that she wished to have it both ways.[22] Without diminishing the contribution that LaCugna has made to recovering a language of the economic Trinity, it must be acknowledged that her construction raises critical issues, and that her work has not proven itself to be the definitive reading of a gendered economy.

Leonardo Boff

Leonardo Boff was a doctoral student of Rahner, a thinker whom Boff describes as the most intelligent and creative theologian of the twentieth century.[23] Yet when Boff employs Rahner's rule in his own Trinitarian construction, he does so with more caution, applying the rule circumspectly.[24] Boff will say in simple terms,

The Blessed Trinity has been revealed in people's lives, in religions, in

---

18. Neil Ormerod, *The Trinity: Retrieving the Western Tradition* (Milwaukee: Marquette University Press, 2005), 24.
19. J. A. DiNoia, review of *God for Us*, by Catherine Mowry LaCugna, *Modern Theology* 9 (1993): 216.
20. Ted Peters, *God as Trinity: Relationality and Temporality in the Divine Life* (Louisville: Westminster John Knox, 1993), 143.
21. Olson and Hall, *The Trinity*, 112.
22. Grenz, *Rediscovering the Triune God*, 161.
23. Leonardo Boff, *When Theology Listens to the Poor*, trans. Robert R. Barr (San Francisco: Harper and Row 1988), x.
24. Grenz, *Rediscovering the Triune God*, 126.

history and then in the life, passion, death and resurrection of Jesus, and through the manifestation of the Holy Spirit in the community of the early church and in the process of history down through our time. . . . The reality of the three divine Persons has always accompanied human history. Doctrine arose later when people grasped the revelation of the Blessed Trinity and were able to formulate trinitarian doctrines.[25]

Yet, unlike Rahner, Boff finds his starting point for Trinitarian reflection in the historical threeness of God (not in God the Father). In doing so, he hopes to avoid both the processional conception of the East and the Western focus on the one God of faith.[26] Boff argues that the rigid monotheism of the West leads to totalitarianism in politics and authoritarianism in religion.[27] He also sees paternalism in society and machismo in the family as a result of father-centred reflection: "The great Lords of this world dominate society and the family by invoking the name of God as 'boss' or 'owner.' They forget that God has a son and lives with the Holy Spirit in perfect equality."[28] Beginning with the Triune revelation, Boff hopes to highlight the oppressive theological underpinnings of society and to present an alternative and liberating account of the Trinity. In his framework, what matters most is the "eternal co-relatedness, the self surrender of each Person to the others."[29] The economic Trinity does not represent, for Boff, "the whole of the immanent Trinity."[30] Boff instead appeals to perichoresis as the basis for his claims of egalitarian relations within the Godhead, and as a way of avoiding

---

25. Leonardo Boff, *Holy Trinity, Perfect Community*, trans. Phillip Berryman (Maryknoll, NY: Orbis, 2000), 16, 17.

26. Of course, there is not a clear distinction for Boff, who never really abandons the language of the West. This is a point noted by Stanley Grenz, who suggests (along with Paul Fiddes) that the Western tradition is far more appealing for Boff's particular liberative motives; Grenz, *Rediscovering the Triune God*, 124.

27. Boff, *Holy Trinity, Perfect Community*, 7, 8.

28. Ibid., 8.

29. Boff, *Trinity and Society*, trans. Paul Burns (Maryknoll, NY: Orbis, 1988), 5.

30. Ibid., 95 and 215.

the dangers of tritheism.[31] Boff regards the perichoretic unity as a unity of love and as perfect personal communion rather than as a unity of substance or of origin.[32] But it is at this point that problems with Boff's Trinitarian framework emerge. First, in order to support this claim of perichoretic equality within the economic Trinity, Boff makes the unusual claim that Father, Son, and Spirit emerge simultaneously, undermining traditional understandings of the divine relations:

> The Father is said to be source and cause of the entire Godhead. From him proceed the Son and the Holy Spirit. The Father is also said to generate the Son. Father and Son spirate the Holy Spirit as from a single principle. These expressions—cause, generation, spiration and processions—may give us the impression that in God there is some sort of theogony. Can we really say that the principal of causality is valid in the Trinity? . . . Do we not always say that the Divine Persons are originally simultaneous, and that they eternally coexist in communion and in interpenetration (perichoresis)?[33]

Understandably, some critics find this suggestion completely unacceptable, and suggest it finds basis neither in Scripture nor tradition.[34] Furthermore, and perhaps this is the most difficult aspect of Boff's "perfect community," is his move to divinize the Virgin Mary. Boff argues (largely from the Lukan narrative), that the Holy Spirit is incarnate in Mary. He suggests, "Mary, then . . . is the true, physical temple of the Holy Spirit, in a way analogous to Jesus as the dwelling place of the eternal Son."[35]

---

31. Boff's conception in some way mirrors the claims of John Zizioulas, who suggests, "The *one* not only does not precede—logically or otherwise—the *many*, but, on the contrary, requires the *many* from the very start in order to exist." See John D. Zizioulas, "The Doctrine of the Holy Trinity: The Significance of the Cappadocian Contribution," in *Trinitarian Theology Today: Essays on Divine Being and Act*, ed. Christoph Schwöbel (Edinburgh: T & T Clark, 1995), 49.

32. Olson and Hall, *The Trinity*, 107.

33. Boff, *Holy Trinity, Perfect Community*, 59.

34. For instance, see Ormerod, *The Trinity*, 26.

Obviously there is a liberating potential in such ideas, yet Boff's Mariology not only goes beyond the teaching of his church, but also suggests an "adoptionist Christology that stands outside the historic teaching of the church as a whole."[36] Further questions need to be asked as to the necessity of such a move. The Mary hypothesis is of such significance that the validity of Boff's whole Trinitarian scheme becomes problematic. The difficulty for Boff is that in seeking to locate a liberating locus of Trinitarian relations within the economic Trinity, he has failed to take seriously the biblical witness to divine procession.[37] Moreover, the notion of perichoresis as a model for ideal community is itself questionable. Kathryn Tanner, for instance, rejects the utopian representation of community modeled on perichoretic unity as a safeguard against oppressive agendas. She argues that trinitarianism can be just as politically dangerous as monotheism,[38] and that we should look to the economy not to model our own communities, but instead to learn from Triune interaction how we too can participate in the divine life.[39] Similarly, in analysis of Boff's efforts to undermine hierarchy, Ted Peters argues that the "perfect community" fails in its endeavors: "Although Boff wants to work with a correlation between a divine society and a human society on a nonhierarchical basis, the divine society of which he

35. Boff, *Holy Trinity, Perfect Community*. And also see his *The Maternal Face of God: The Feminine and Its Religious Experience*, trans. Robert R. Barr and John W. Dierksmeire (San Francisco: Harper and Row, 1987).
36. Grenz, *Rediscovering the Triune God*, 129, 130.
37. Though Boff clearly asserts this "simultaneous emergence," he never completely divorces himself from traditional language. Instead, he suggests that the processional language of the church should be used in an "analogous and figurative sense'." In addition, it is ironic that one of Boff's major metaphors for the economic Trinity is his utilization of Irenaeus's "two hands of God" (of which Jesus and the now *pneumatized* Mary become the hands of the Father), which could certainly be interpreted as a classic example of hierarchy and procession. See Boff, *Holy Trinity, Perfect Community*, 59 and 16.
38. Kathryn Tanner, "Trinity," in *The Blackwell Companion to Political Theology*, ed. William T. Cavanaugh and Peter Scott (Oxford: Blackwell, 2003), 323.
39. Ibid., 328, 329.

speaks is in fact a monarchy; and because this monarchy is shrouded in eternal mystery apart from the time in which we live, no genuine correlation with human society can be made."[40]

Gavin D'Costa

Gavin D'Costa aims explicitly to explore concepts of gender and patriarchy within the Godhead. In *Sexing the Trinity*,[41] D'Costa does not structure his theology in a typical systematic fashion, yet he provides a good example of contemporary scholarship seeking to destabilize gender within Trinitarian discourse, especially in light of Irigaray's theoretical work. D'Costa begins by surveying Irigaray's stinging critique on both language and the Christian church. Irigaray's interest in the Trinity[42] is obviously of interest to D'Costa. He is aware that feminizing the Spirit may not only relegate the feminine to an eternally subordinate position, but that it also "ironically highlights the taxonomies of representation that have tended to exist in both east and west and which have subjugated the Spirit in symbolically equal terms to the subjugation of women in western culture."[43] Yet he still argues for the validity of Irigaray's demands for sexual difference within the Godhead. In order to defend this claim, D'Costa appeals to Thomas Weinandy's argument[44] that the Aristotelian prioritization of Father and Son within the divine being have led to a deformed subjectivity of the Spirit. As Weinandy suggests,

---

40. Peters, *God as Trinity*, 114.
41. Gavin D'Costa, *Sexing the Trinity: Gender, Culture and the Divine* (London: SCM, 2000).
42. Particularly drawing on Luce Irigaray, "Equal to Whom," in *The Postmodern God*, ed. Graham Ward (Oxford: Blackwell, 1997).
43. D'Costa, *Sexing the Trinity*, 11.
44. Thomas Weinandy, *The Father's Spirit of Sonship: Reconceiving the Trinity* (Edinburgh: T & T Clark, 1995).

For the West, the Father and (derivatively) the Son play active roles within the Trinity. In contrast, the Holy Spirit assumes a rather passive function. The Spirit is merely the Love or Gift shared by the Father and Son. It is therefore difficult to see why, in the western conception of the Trinity, the Holy Spirit is a distinct person or subject.[45]

Weinandy also levels his critique against the East for rendering the full subjectivity of the Spirit in highly problematic fashion (because of its linear construct and portrayal of fatherly monarchy).[46] D'Costa uses these critiques to move Trinitarian theology in the direction of Iragaray. He writes,

> Reading Weinandy through Irigaraian lenses helps to locate a tenuous link between the inchoate subjectivity of the Holy Spirit, the underdetermined "subjectivity" of women, and the lack of divine feminine representation. At first sight, the one person of the Trinity who might bear feminine gendering is also the person who has the most diminished subjectivity and lack of personhood.[47]

What follows for D'Costa is similar to Boff: reaching out to Mary as a potential figure of emancipation. Yet D'Costa is critical of Boff for "postulating a singular and unique hypostatisation of the Spirit in Mary."[48] In contrast, D'Costa argues that Mary provides a model for the divinization of all creation (along with other women of Israel and history who indeed function as coredeemers).[49] It is this cult of women saints and coredeemers that D'Costa hopes will provide the "imaginary whereby women's subjectivity may be attained in multiple forms."[50] Yet the distinction here is that gender has not become essentialized; in fact, D'Costa points to the greater gender fluidity of the Godhead represented within the tradition. Citing

45. Ibid., 8.
46. Ibid., 236.
47. D'Costa, *Sexing the Trinity*, 19.
48. Ibid., 26.
49. Ibid., 27.
50. Ibid., 39.

Syrian sources, he shows that careful exegesis of certain Syrian worshiping communities points to both the essential fluidity of gender and the destabilizing of language itself in the event of the incarnation.[51] Hence, D'Costa criticizes Irigaray for freezing notions of gender and body in the person of Jesus. In emphasizing Jesus' relationship to Mary,[52] D'Costa argues that the particularity of the incarnation is precisely the vehicle to transgress gender and render Irigaray's demands redundant. The same fluidity, according to D'Costa,[53] may be found in the biblical Father who is semantically transgressive and "has nothing to do with origins."[54] Indeed, "this delightful transgression confounds those who want to control symbols."[55]

D'Costa's engagement with a variety of disciplines and his critical response to Irigaray are creative and timely. Yet in rejecting patriarchy in the Godhead, D'Costa has ended up with the same problems that confront Boff's proposal. The radical symmetrizing of the relations of persons within the Trinity lacks scriptural or traditional support.[56] When D'Costa does appeal to biblical sources, his scant exegesis raises more questions than it answers.[57] A similar critique has been made of D'Costa's exegesis of patristic sources relating to divine fatherhood.[58] Further, D'Costa seems to draw on various models of Mariology that at times contradict or at least subvert each other. In the final analysis, his thesis does not resolve

51. Ibid., 45.
52. On this occasion, drawing from the work of Tina Beattie.
53. Now utilizing Paul Ricoeur.
54. D'Costa, *Sexing the Trinity*, 94.
55. Ibid., 75.
56. Ormerod, *The Trinity*, 26.
57. A point raised by Esther D. Reed, review of *Sexing the Trinity: Gender, Culture and the Divine*, by Gavin D'Costa, *Reviews in Religion & Theology* 8, no. 4 (2001): 416.
58. Sarah Coakley, review of *Sexing the Trinity: Gender, Culture and the Divine*, by Gavin D'Costa, *Theology & Sexuality: The Journal of the Institute for the Study of Christianity & Sexuality* 11, no. 3 (2005): 92.

the question of gender in the Trinity. While he painstakingly argues for cases of gender fluidity within the tradition, he also speaks of a multigendered reality. One is left unsure how this proposal responds to the critique of Irigaray regarding binaries.

Kevin J. Vanhoozer and an Incorporative Model of the Trinity

Kevin Vanhoozer might seem an unlikely ally for a feminist theology of the Trinity; but in this section, I want to argue that Vanhoozer's work provides a more promising approach to problems of difference and gender in Trinitarian discourse. Vanhoozer develops the hypothesis that it is in fact a doctrine of the Trinity that helps us to develop a coherent doctrine of Scripture.[59] In this regard, he cites Lewis Ayres: "Scripture tells the story of the Triune God in which the Father reaches down with both hands, Son and Spirit, so that we can reach back to God."[60] Despite the doctrines of God and Scripture drifting apart throughout much of the church's history, Vanhoozer credits Karl Barth for taking the first steps in bringing the doctrines back together. Yet for Vanhoozer, Nicholas Wolterstorff's critique of Barth raises critical issues that require resolution if the Trinity is to resolve the problematic nature of the doctrine of Scripture. Wolterstorff argues that Barth limits the divine speech act to a stretch of history and not to a stretch of language; further, Barth ascribes the utterance of God to Jesus Christ and not to Scripture; and finally, the Barthian account of revelation is said to have nothing to do with Scripture but only to the revealed event in the life of the interpreter.[61]

---

59. Kevin J. Vanhoozer, "Theological Reflections on the Claim That God Speaks (Part 1)," in *Trinitarian Theology for the Church*, ed. Daniel J. Treier and David Lauber (Downers Grove, IL: InterVarsity, 2009).

60. Lewis Ayres, "On the Practice and Teaching of Christian Doctrine," *Gregorianum* 80 (1999): 44.

61. Nicholas Wolterstorff, *Divine Discourse: Philosophical Reflections on the Claim That God Speaks* (Cambridge: Cambridge University Press, 1995), 68–72.

What is required in response to these problems, Vanhoozer suggests, is a theology of divine discourse on christological and pneumalogical grounds—that is, a doctrine of the Trinity as a doctrinal explanation of the way God speaks in Scripture.

In examining the pervasive biblical theme of divine discourse, and in tying this to the incarnation, Vanhoozer argues,

> The incarnation thus serves as a check on our tendency to play divine transcendence off against human language. Furthermore, if the incarnate Son of God can speak our words, it follows that we have at least one instance of literal divine speech: "When Jesus opens his mouth and speaks Scripture, . . . Barth's distinction evaporates." These words do not become but are the word of God. The line between divine and discourse is breached: the infinite intones.[62]

Vanhoozer, committed to the rule that the economic interaction reveals the immanent Trinity, argues that the discourse between the Father, Son, and Spirit reveals that God's being is in conversation. The key moments of dialogue within the Triune economy represent the communicative face of divine perichoresis. "God's being [is] essentially communicative and the three persons [are] a dialogue between communicative agents."[63] Vanhoozer builds on this with a rhetorical analogy, thus combining both social and psychological analogies—a deft way of avoiding either tritheism or modalism. Each person of the Trinity, he suggests, "appropriates a certain rhetorical function to Himself: the Father takes responsibility for the ethos of discourse, the Son for the logos of discourse and the Spirit for the pathos of discourse."[64] Vanhoozer's proposal is that divine communication is thus "a unified action with three dimensions," so that Scripture is in turn best understood "not as divinely appropriated

---

62. Vanhoozer, "Theological Reflections on the Claim That God Speaks (Part 2)," in Treier and Lauber, *Trinitarian Theology for the Church*, 54.
63. Ibid., 58.
64. Ibid., 62.

human discourse, but [as] human discourse that from start to finish is caught up in the field of divine communicative action."[65] In Vanhoozer's model, the persons of the Trinity address the speaker's moral character (the ethos of God the Father), the basic message and its means of utterance (the logos of the Son), and the effect upon the listener (the pathos of the Spirit)—so that Scripture is grounded in the divine economy. Drawing on this creative proposal, I want to show that we also find here surprising resources for responding to the complexities of gender within the economic Trinity.

A rhetorical analogy maintains a sense of mystery and balances the apophatic with the positive content of revelation in the divine economy. The Trinity does not collapse into history; this analogy speaks of the God who enters into history to invite us back into divine communion (consequently securing divine freedom). "The Triune God ultimately deploys Scripture as a means of expanding the inner-trinitarian conversation and hence the circle of his friendly conversation."[66] This is the communicative face of perichoresis. Further, Vanhoozer's decision to begin not with our static human situation (as might be said of Boff) but from *above*, in the dynamic of the divine persons in the economy, provides a more coherent way of understanding emancipation. The communicative face of perichoresis draws the listener into the key moments of the divine economy: Are those seeking liberative models of the Trinity looking to God from the wrong side of history?

A rhetorical model also provides a unique avenue into the prickly issues of procession, hierarchy, and subordination within the Godhead. Vanhoozer's analogy of ethos, logos, and pathos suggests equality within the Godhead, and seems to avoid echoes of subordinationism. Though Vanhoozer does not explicitly challenge

65. Ibid., 59.
66. Ibid., 67.

the notion of procession (which may disappoint some feminists), there is a sense of symmetry in his emphasis on the efficacy, or the pathos, of the Spirit. By placing the "success" of divine speech in the hands of the Spirit, the oppressive structures of origin and procession are dismantled, while power is placed in the hands of precisely that which undermines rigid binaries: the *third*. It is here that a rhetorical model stands up to Sarah Coakley's challenge to contemporary theology.

Coakley has argued that it is contemplative practice that disrupts the gender binaries we assume as either fixed or to be abolished. This, of course, relates to contemplative practice in which one welcomes the destabilizing Holy Spirit. Coakley interprets the Spirit as a means of incorporation into the Triune life.[67] Reading Romans 8, she describes the way the Trinity allures and transforms creation.[68] She also hints at the potential of trinitarianism to dismantle the patriarchal hierarchy associated with many models of the Trinity. Here a doctrinal trinitarian perspective is brought to bear on conceptions of creaturely difference. For Coakley, it is the third person of the Godhead who holds the key to disrupting power and drawing us away from oppressive structures. In Vanhoozer's rhetorical analogy one finds a similar model of incorporative pneumatology: "The *pathos* of Scripture reminds us that God's speech solicits our participation in the communicative economy."[69] From this incorporative perspective, one may see gender and difference being drawn into the purgative and transformative presence of the Triune God. We are swept up into

---

67. Sarah Coakley, "Why Three? Some Further Reflections on the Origins on the Doctrine of the Trinity," in *The Making and Remaking of Christian Doctrine: Essays in Honour of Maurice Wiles*, ed. Maurice F. Wiles, Sarah Coakley, and David A. Pailin (Oxford: Oxford University Press, 1993), 29–56.
68. Ibid., 37.
69. Vanhoozer, "Theological Reflections on the Claim That God Speaks (Part 2)," 66.

the life of the Trinity by the agency of the Spirit, so that, in Coakley's words, "twoness . . . is divinely ambushed by threeness."[70]

70. Coakley, "Is There a Future for Gender and Theology? On Gender, Contemplation, and the Systematic Task," *Criterion* 47, no. 1 (2009): 11.

7

———

Struggled For and Not Possessed

Language for the Triune God and the Apophatic Turn

Naming God has enormous discursive power. The implications of "masculine" terminology for God were foundational for second-wave feminism. Understandably, feminist theologians have sought to destabilize the gender rigidity of language about God. And yet feminist rearticulations often bring with them the same discursive rules that are criticized in the use of masculine language. When women's experience becomes the basis of language for God, feminists risk ascribing a fixed symbol upon the divine name. However, in practices of prayer and contemplation the sheer otherness of God draws us to the limits of language, and causes a blurring of all fixed linguistic boundaries.

Religious Language, Feminism and God

In a recent essay, William Alston poses the question, "Do you speak English, French, or religious?"[1] Linguists observe that any given language has all the resources it needs to talk about all topics. For Alston, philosophy's tendency to speak of special language for special subject matter (e.g., the language of physics) fails to take seriously the distinction between language and speech.[2] Yet despite technical distinctions, the term *religious language* is well entrenched in connection to the whole spectrum of religious practice, so entrenched that even Alston agrees to continue the use of this terminology. Whether language is of the so-called religious variety or not, feminist theologians also know a thing or two about the entrenchment of words and signs. Well before the arrival of second-wave feminism, Elizabeth Cady Stanton famously removed all of what she perceived to be patriarchal language from the Bible in her 1898 publication of *The Women's Bible*.[3] Similar examinations of the texts of Christian tradition have been made, exposing obvious cases of misogyny in the language of the church.[4] The ongoing analysis of language by feminists reflects their clear understanding of what is at stake, especially in regard to language for the divine. As Elizabeth Johnson notes,

> [In] speech the symbol of God functions as the primary symbol of the whole religious system, the ultimate point of reference for understanding experience, life and the world. Hence the way in which a faith based community shapes language about God implicitly represents

1. William P Alston, "Religious Language," in *The Oxford Handbook of Philosophy of Religion*, ed. William J. Wainwright (Oxford: Oxford University Press, 2005), 31.
2. Ibid., 220.
3. Second-wave projects seek to look below and within the text for the contribution of women and find meaning in the hidden and subsumed voices. For instance, see the work of Elizabeth Schüssler Fiorenza and Phyllis Trible.
4. A fine example is the partnered project of Elizabeth Moltmann-Wendel and Jürgen Moltmann, *Humanity in God* (Cleveland: Pilgrim, 1983).

what it takes to be the highest good, the profoundest truth, the most appealing beauty.[5]

Johnson is not alone in emphasizing the imperative function of language. She joins company with the growing number of thinkers who recognize the critical implications "that speech about God carries not only for human theological knowledge but also for social relations and even for the future of life on earth."[6]

Feminists have employed various responses to the problems of language. A common theme is the attempted elimination of dualistic language with its concomitant diminishment of women. This language is said to bolster hierarchy and to place damning divisions within the created order.[7] Rebecca Chopp's constructive response insists that in order to change this monotheistic ordering, women must "multiply the possible signifiers and enrich the signifying process."[8] Chopp's work represents a critical attempt to fashion an open symbol, the "Word," in relation to feminist theological semiotics, and consequently to give women the power to speak. Metaphor, too, has become an area of significant research, especially through the influence of Sallie McFague's work. McFague's concern reflects the desire for metaphors "appropriate for our time."[9] More radically, in the early decades, Mary Daly suggestively rebirthed words to create new meaning(s) within the matrix of womenspeak.[10]

5. Johnson, *She Who Is: The Mystery of God in Feminist Theological Discourse*, 10th anniversary ed. (New York: Crossroad, 1992), 4.

6. Grenz, *Rediscovering the Triune God: The Trinity in Contemporary Theology* (Minneapolis: Fortress Press, 2004), 166.

7. L. Isherwood and D. McEwan, *Introducing Feminist Theology*, 2nd ed. (Sheffield: Sheffield Academic, 2001), 118.

8. Rebecca S. Chopp, *The Power to Speak: Feminism, Language, God* (New York: Crossroad, 1989), 3.

9. McFague, *Models of God: Theology for an Ecological, Nuclear Age* (Philadelphia: Fortress Press, 1987), 13.

10. See Daly, *Beyond God the Father: Toward a Philosophy of Women's Liberation* (Boston: Beacon, 1973).

Today, feminist theology is attempting to tease apart the complexities of subjectivity in relationship to language, particularly with theories about the undecidability of meaning.[11] Recent comparisons have been made between Anglo-American feminism (which reaches for equality in life through the vehicle of language), and the French approach, concerned with the repression of the feminine in language and symbol.[12] In this context of analysis and revision, feminist theology has welcomed the apophatic turn. One can see why those striving for an end to patriarchal discourse would see the flourishing of apophatic discourse as an important resource.

In this chapter, I will suggest that a tension exists regarding feminist theology's relationship with apophasis and language for the divine. Feminist theology (and not only feminist theology) often finds itself affirming the absolute poverty of language while simultaneously viewing language as the key to women's emancipation. What's more, and perhaps more difficult to situate, this kind of constructive work is often done within a latent empirical framework that proves incongruous with the apophatic sensibilities that are advocated. In this chapter, I wish to explore this tension, and to argue that properly apophatic language for God is possible and that apophasis does indeed point toward an open and fluid language for the Triune God.

11. Mary McClintock Fulkerson notes that in this area poststructuralisms differ: "Some concern language with Saussure as forebear (Derrida), others are connected with language, but focus more on desire (Lacan, Focault)." See Mary McClintock Fulkerson, "Feminist Theology," in *The Cambridge Companion to Postmodern Theology*, ed. Kevin J. Vanhoozer (Cambridge: Cambridge University Press, 2003), 114.
12. Janet Martin Soskice, *The Kindness of God: Metaphor, Gender, and Religious Language* (Oxford: Oxford University Press, 2007), 107.

The Apophatic in Feminist Discourse

Feminist theology has long been attuned to the theme of apophasis. William Franke notes that feminist discourse tends to be "exceptionally fecund in reflection about silence and its significances."[13] Scholars have welcomed the potential of apophasis to empower and enliven feminist theology. Anne Carr, in *Transforming Grace*, retrieves the classic notion of incomprehensibility, acknowledging that she is not in the end able to say what God is.[14] Catherine Mowry LaCugna calls the ineffability of God axiomatic in theology,[15] and Elizabeth Johnson shows how apophatic tendencies are uncovering "the false assumptions that underlie insistence on exclusively male language and thereby propelling new discovery of holy mystery which we call God."[16] Jacqueline daCosta even writes about the possibility of apophatic theology for the Goddess.[17] For many feminists, language, particularly language about God, is considered to be "set free"[18] through apophaticism. Thus apophatic sensibilities are used by a wide variety of feminists to defend revisionist language about the divine, and especially feminine names for the Triune God. Johnson would exhort her reader to employ a polyphony of names for God, not only as legitimate but as necessary.[19] But in utilizing such language for God, the feminist is

13. Of course, as Franke notes, the bulk of this early writing pertains to the silencing of female voices and focused "sharply on class, colour, and sex as motives for the silencing." See William Franke, *On What Cannot Be Said: Apophatic Discourses in Philosophy, Religion, Literature, and the Arts*, vol. 2. (Notre Dame: University of Notre Dame Press, 2007), 5.

14. Anne E. Carr, *Transforming Grace: Christian Tradition and Women's Experience* (San Francisco: Harper & Row, 1988).

15. LaCugna, *God For Us* (New York: Harper Collins, 1991), 323.

16. Johnson, *She Who Is*, 112.

17. See Jacqueline daCosta, "Can Apophatic Theology Be Applied to Goddessing as Well as to God?," *Feminist Theology: The Journal of the Britain & Ireland School of Feminist Theology* 11, no. 1 (2002): 82–98.

18. Johnson, *She Who Is*, 112.

19. Ibid., 120.

simply reperforming the gender binary linguistically (to use Butlerian terms). And in seeking to image God as a woman, appeals to the *via negativa* are surely ironic; apparently women are supposed to feel a sense of identification with a God who is (by definition) not at all like them! Furthermore, what we find at work in much of this feminist construction is a concealed empiricism operating beneath the formal claims for apophatism.

Sallie McFague, for example, asserts the radical mystery of God and argues that all talk of God is indirect,[20] yet she is famous for insisting that all naming of God is contextually bound and so tied to the tests and trials of lived experience. The *is* component of her definition for metaphor (for McFague a metaphor always displays an *is* and *is not* function) has been critiqued as propagating an essentially realist conception of God.[21] Similarly, Elizabeth Johnson argues that the symbol of God inevitably functions not only in the religious community, but throughout the entire cosmos. Because this symbol yields so much power, we must ensure that it functions in a way that does not exclude women. As Paul Molnar has noted, "The suggestion clearly is that it is we who invest the symbol with meaning and it is we who thus must change the symbol in order to obtain the desired social result."[22] The desired results for women's emancipation come from women's experience and thus it is women's experience that defines the symbol, providing a kind of check against the possibility of divine ineffability. Another interesting challenge emerges in the discussion of apophaticism and the whole idea of experience. With the well-documented emphasis on women's experience in feminist

20. McFague, *Models of God*, 34.
21. A critique made by Coakley, "Feminist Theology," in *Modern Christian Thought*, vol. 2, *The Twentieth Century*, ed. James C. Livingston et al. (Minneapolis: Fortress Press, 2006), 432.
22. Paul D. Molnar, *Divine Freedom and the Doctrine of the Immanent Trinity: In Dialogue with Karl Barth and Contemporary Theology* (Edinburgh: T & T Clark, 2002), 9. Cited in Grenz, *Rediscovering the Triune God*, 178.

theology, one might wonder how a system of "unknowing" can come to bear on lived experience. Given the historical importance of naming one's experience within this tradition, the concept of surrendering the possibility of such naming, or indeed even the knowledge of the experience, would no doubt prove threatening. Still, it does seem that such a possibility could provide insight into the endless debates about the starting point and qualifications for women writing feminist theology.

Once a system has been established around such a clear governing principle (such as "personality" or "radical mystery" or whatever) the extent to which the system is truly apophatic must be questioned. This is not to suggest that we smugly choose silence to protect ourselves from the obvious risks (a move that Gunton is right to criticize[23]) or that, conceptually, apophasis is without its own proper tensions and contradictions. Indeed, even to assert that something is ineffable is a contradiction in terms. Yet these examples pose a challenge for apophatic theology in relation to language about God and its relationship to feminist theology.

Apophatic Discourse and the Mystics

In William Franke's two-volume anthology *On What Cannot Be Said*, we are presented with the pervasiveness of apophatic discourse "throughout the history of European and American thought and art."[24] In developing this narrative,[25] Franke helps us to see in

23. Colin E. Gunton, *The Promise of Trinitarian Theology* (Edinburgh: T & T Clark, 1991), 193.
24. Scott Bailey, review of *On What Cannot Be Said: Apophatic Discourses in Philosophy, Religion, Literature, and the Arts*, by William Franke, *Christianity & Literature* 59, no. 2 (2010): 374.
25. Bruce Milem critiques Franke for his, at times, uncritical explication of apophaticism, suggesting that Franke fails to take seriously the interplay of Logos and *via negativa* in some of the authors he includes (such as Aquinas). See Bruce Milem, review of *On What Cannot Be Said: Apophatic Discourses in Philosophy, Religion, Literature and the Arts*, by William Franke *Heythrop Journal* 51, no. 1 (2010): 174–75.

particular the importance of apophatic language in the development of the doctrine of God. In the minds of the Neoplatonists, "the *via negativa* emerges as a way to render possible a discourse about transcendent realities, especially 'The One,' for which all positive expressions are found to be inadequate."[26] With his comprehensive historical survey of apophatic texts, Franke is attempting to theorize apophatic discourse and to present a theory of what it means to speak of the "The One." Notably, Franke's overarching thesis is that apophatic discourse, while present since antiquity, has been silenced by a Western obsession with the Logos. He suggests that it is at times when faith in the Logos is in crisis that apophatic discourse flourishes.[27]

Franke credits Dionysius the Areopagate with forging a new configuration in apophatic thought. In bringing together the Neoplatonic heritage of negation with biblical revelation and theology, the revealed God of Christianity becomes God of ineffability. Franke writes of Dionysius's works: "In these writings . . ., the same logic of negating all predications is applied, just as in the Neoplatonic *via negativa*, but it is no longer simply the One that is unsayable so much as the Creator God of the Christian Scriptures, the Trinity."[28] In this radical reinterpretation of the Neoplatonic ineffable one,[29] new possibilities and challenges emerge in the discourse of the unsayable; the focus is no longer exclusively on a remote

---

26. William Franke, *On What Cannot Be Said*, 1:9.

27. Ibid., 31.

28. Franke does note that this new way has been prepared for "well in advance by Christian predecessors, such as Clement of Alexandria, Gregory of Nyssa, and John Chrysostom." See ibid., 13.

29. Franke also provides and extensive explanation of the collapse of the Neoplatonic hypostasis of both the *One* and *Being* as unsayable. Such thinking is said to "open the experience in time in the direction of an absolute which can become real as event and revelation in history." Thus human and knowledge and language are assessed in relation to their dependency of what cannot be said. This explanation provides a response to the popular philosophical objections to metaphysics that claims we must "adhere to the surface of what can be said." Ibid., 26.

transcendent Other, but on a mystery somehow present and revealed. Franke traces this marriage in thought back through all Abrahamic religions and especially notes its manifestation in the mystic effusions of Kabbalah and Sufism. "Only a mystical link can exist between the manifest world and this inner, secret 'region' or divine 'reality.'"[30] In the writing of Maimonides, Aquinas, and ultimately in Eckhart, the ineffable Being is seen to be in the presence of all beings and takes on a distinctly existential edge. Consequently, apophatic discourse serves a method of spiritual unmastery:

> There can be, then, some knowledge of the right ways of relating to and even of speaking about God, though they can give us no objective information about him. Analogy gives no scientific knowledge of God as an object. And yet our ways of experiencing our own limits vis-a-vis the infinity of God are revealing of the God we do not know but relate to—precisely in encountering these limits and, simultaneously, in abandoning our pretensions to knowledge. While there can be no knowledge of God, our knowledge as creatures as inadequate analogies for him can lead to unknowing, that is to Eckhart's *unwizzen*. . . . The analogies operate then, really, as disanloagies: it is not their content, but rather the spilling over of all bounds of content, their *uncontainement*, that conveys something, some inkling of God.[31]

Such apophatic language and experience, I believe, has important potential for feminist theology, and for the way women, through apophatic practices, may engage in "untelling" us of the Triune God.[32] It is through such practices that one is drawn to the limits of theology. Indeed, we might say, with Gregory Palamas, that such

---

30. Ibid., 14.

31. Ibid, 30

32. Another aspect of Franke's historical thesis that may prove fruitful in theological discussion is his account of Jewish philosopher Franz Rosenzweig. Rosenzweig's theory of apophatic grammar known as "speaking-thinking" focuses on relationality and bears some significance in the discussion of language for the Triune God. Consider, for instance, Rahner's doctrine of divine mystery and its implications for the naming of the economic Trinity. See Franke, *On What Cannot Be Said* for a clearer picture of Franke's account of Rosenzweig's significance.

experience is beyond negation.[33] To return once more to Dionysius: "The fact is that the more we take upward flight, the more our words are confided to the ideas we are capable of forming, so that now as we plunge into the darkness which is beyond intellect, we shall find ourselves not simply running short of words but actually speechless."[34]

It is in the spiritual practices of negation and unmastery that language takes on this unique dimension. Janet Martin Soskice makes similar claims about the apophatic experience in her technical evaluation of religious language and metaphor.[35] Soskice's main concern is to define metaphor and its function in order to defend its validity in religious discourse.[36] Yet along the way, she notes the transgressive power of language when embedded in experience:

> All the metaphors which we use to speak of God arise from experiences of that which cannot be adequately described, of that which Jews and Christian believe to be "He who Is." The apophatic is always present with the cataphatic and we are most in danger of theological travesty when we forget this is so.[37]

As an example of this unknowing, Soskice turns to John Donne's poem "A Hymn to Christ, at the Author's Last Going into Germany." In this poem, it is both the absence and presence of God that expose the uncertainty and the limits of experience. For Soskice, this is no less than "the beginning and end of theology."[38] As the poem reaches its conclusion, Donne leads his reader—as Soskice points out—to, prayer, darkness and silence.[39] Donne writes,

33. Franke, *On What Cannot Be Said*, vol.1,1.
34. Dionysius, *Complete Works* (1033B–C) cited in ibid., 16–17.
35. Janet Martin Soskice, *Metaphor and Religious Language* (Oxford: Clarendon, 1985).
36. Soskice suggests that in analyzing how metaphor works, she may be able to show what a theological realism vis-a-vis metaphor might actually look like. Ibid.
37. Ibid., 160.
38. Ibid.
39. Ibid., 161.

Churches are best for Prayer, that have least light:
To see God only, I goe out of sight:
And to scape stormy dayes, I chuse
An Everlasting night.[40]

In several essays on the doctrine of God,[41] Soskice draws out this theme more in reference to the mystic Julian of Norwich. Though Julian's *Shewings* "make uncomfortable reading in a world unaccustomed to visions," the work is also, Soskice argues, a deeply considered essay on the doctrine of the Trinity.[42] This view has been defended recently by Denys Turner, who reads Julian's *Shewings* as a work of systematic theology.[43] Fittingly, this theology really serves as a spiritual exercise. Julian begins her final chapter with the words, "This book is begun by God's gift and his grace, and is not yet performed as I see it."[44] And so the language of Julian's trinitarianism is paired with a willing epistemological vulnerability. She writes,

As truly as God is our Father, so truly is God our mother, and he revealed that in everything, and especially these sweet words, where he says, I am he, the power and goodness of fatherhood; I am he, the wisdom and lovingness of motherhood; I am he, the light and grace which is all blessed love.[45]

Here we find metaphor operating its most open and fluid sense. Gender does not become a fixed point of differentiation within the Trinity, yet the apophatic dynamic of the language achieves a remarkable transgression of gender binaries.

---

40. John Donne, *A Hymne to Christ, at the Author's Last Going into Germany.*
41. Soskice, *The Kindness of God.*
42. Ibid., 125.
43. Denys Turner, *Julian of Norwich, Theologian* (London: Yale University Press, 2011).
44. (S86), cited in Soskice, *The Kindness of God*, 155.
45. Julian of Norwich, *Showings*, trans. Edmund Colledge and James Walsh, Classics of Western Spirituality. (New York: Paulist, 1978), chap 59, 256–59. Cited in Soskice, *The Kindness of God*, 116.

Speaking of the Triune God

William Alston has pointed to the need for attention to the way language functions in spiritual practices. He notes that philosophers have been narrowly selective in their study of religious traditions: dominated "for the most part by epistemological and metaphysical concerns, they have concentrated on what look to be factual statements about God."[46] Yet the language associated with apophatic practice reveals quite different possibilities, and functions in quite different ways from the language of technical rational precision. Yet the question of gender still remains for the feminist. Though we must generally agree that theology today is written with a much greater awareness of how gendered language functions and why it matters,[47] a good deal of Trinitarian theology has surfaced in the past decades that seems to ignore the problems of gendered language. It is clear that the Christian theological tradition includes its own resources for a language for God at once orthodox and transgressive of gender binaries; yet such resources are still strangely neglected in much writing on the doctrine of God.

As Franke demonstrates, the history of apophatic discourse coincides with the development of Trinitarian doctrine.[48] The church fathers, in developing the doctrine of the Trinity, above all were conscious of the inadequacy of the formulas.[49] The nature and name of God was a point of consuming interest to medieval mystics (for example Teresa of Avila), and the more recent philosophical

46. Alston, "Religious Language," 221.
47. Isherwood and McEwan give the amusing and yet worrying example of a British MP, who upon hearing of a feminist liturgical publication, declared it "unlawful to change the gender of GOD without Parliamentary consent." Isherwood and McEwan, *Introducing Feminist Theology*, 119.
48. Franke cites Jean Luc Marion as contributing to the discussion of this historical reality. See Franke, "*On What Cannot Be Said*, 34.
49. Johnson, *She Who Is*, 108.

deconstruction of the concept of *name* demonstrates the continuing fascination with the name of God. It is, perhaps, in our struggle to speak of language for God that we become most aware of linguistic limits and our own speechlessness. This becomes most apparent in spiritual and contemplative practices. Karl Rahner suggested that our "interpretation of the mysterious character of the Trinity and of its doctrinal expression entails that not every statement made about the Trinity should be submitted to the premature impatience of the rationalist and of the 'kerygmatist' of mere verbalisms."[50] Rahner believed that true statements or language for the Trinity emerges in the life that participates in faith and grace, not in precise linguistic strategies. It is not surprising, then, that so many scholars today are turning to the Fathers and the mystics to explore the apophatic dimensions of religious language.

Sarah Coakley's retrieval of patristic thought has focused especially on the figure of Gregory of Nyssa. Criticizing current trends in the discussion of the Cappadocian idea of personhood, Coakley examines Gregory of Nyssa's profound apophatic sensibilities as these relate to his Trinitarian language.[51] She argues that in Gregory we find "a strong accompanying sense of the finally inexpressible nature of the divine; as such, the metaphorical status of the language does not detract from the realistic seriousness of the claim, but merely draws our attention to what we can 'nail down' linguistically where God is concerned."[52] Coakley observes that the number three or the concept of number cannot strictly apply to God.[53] In the *Ad Ablabium*, Gregory argues that three does not strictly apply to the

---

50. Rahner, *The Trinity*, 48.
51. Sarah Coakley, "'Persons' in the 'Social' Doctrine of the Trinity: Current Analytic Discussion and 'Cappadocian' Theology," in *Powers and Submissions: Spirituality, Philosophy and Gender*, Challenges in Contemporary Theology (Oxford: Blackwell, 2002), 112.
52. Coakley, "Persons in the Social Doctrine of the Trinity: A Critique of Current Analytic Discussion," in *The Incarnation: An Interdisciplinary Symposium on the Incarnation of the Son of God*, ed. Stephen T. Davis et al. (Oxford: Oxford University Press, 2002), 126.

divine hypostasis. Further, Gregory's favorite analogies for the Trinity—spring, chain, rainbow—stress fluidity at the boundaries between the divine "persons." Gregory's strong apophatic sensibility attaches to whatever he says about essence. Coakley stresses that we find, especially in his *Commentary on the Song of Songs*, "a wealth of discussion regarding the dark 'incomprehensibility' of the divine nature."[54] All of this points to a rather nuanced linguistic method at work in Gregory's language for God.[55] Coakley critiques the common neglect of Gregory's work on "trinitarian spirituality of human transformation," especially his commentary on the *Songs*. It is in this material, his most apophatic and spiritually driven, that Coakley suggests we find the deepest implications for gender: "The gender fluidity that Gregory charts at the human level of transformation finds also its metaphysical counterpart . . . in God."[56] Coakley shows that in the *Songs* and elsewhere, Gregory uses a gendered vocabulary to speak of God, a language intrinsic to the epistemological deepening and transformation that Gregory seeks to convey.[57]

The fluidity of language in these texts provides a unique means of drawing a language of difference into a deepening experience of God's otherness. Patriarchal and other oppressive structures are gently subverted. The most promising resources for such unsettling

---

53. Far from undermining any previous claims regarding the unsettling of binaries through God's "threeness," the way in which three—as a number and concept of logic—is itself subverted through appeals to the apophatic merely demonstrates the plasticity of Triune formulations.

54. Coakley, "Persons in the Social Doctrine of the Trinity: A Critique of Current Analytic Discussion," 122.

55. According to Coakley, on an experiential ordering, we might say that Gregory starts with the Holy Spirit. In *Ad Ablabium*, we are presented with a sense that the Holy Spirit orients our flow into the life of the Trinity. Here we are once again pointed to the intimate connection between pneumatology and apophasis. Hence an ongoing development of pneumatology is required to fully engage with the implications of language, gender, and the Trinity.

56. Coakley, "Persons in the Social Doctrine of the Trinity: A Critique of Current Analytic Discussion," 128.

57. Ibid.

discourse might be found not in the framework of women's experience but instead in practices of spiritual askesis. It is here that language for God is freed from the strictures of empiricism, and space is created for the open and fluid symbol. Experience alone (regardless of which identity politics is involved) cannot become the test or proof of God language; when it does, the apophatic is denied, and the boundaries remain fixed. It is as we are drawn into the destabilizing life of the Triune God that our language is undone.

In A. S. Byatt's novel *Possession*, the poet Randolph Henry Ash senses such an undoing. When he writes to his lover Christabel LaMotte, he says,

> But I go too fast. And I cannot, I must not burden you with a complete confession of what are in any case a very confused, very incoherent, very inchoate set of ideas, perceptions, half-truths, useful fictions, struggled for and not possessed.[58]

---

58. A. S. Byatt, *Possession* (London: Vintage, 2009), 164.

8

———

Subject to Spirit

The Promise of Pentecostal Feminist Pneumatology

I have already explored the way questions surrounding the reality and dignity of creaturely difference are inextricably linked to conceptions of the subject. While previously arguing that theological accounts of freedom and subjectivity must be cast in reference to the sovereignty of God, more must be said about the possibility of subjectivity for those made objects by normative "mankind." In this regard, the emergence of feminist Pentecostal studies poses a sharp challenge to both systematic theology and gender studies. The experiences of Pentecostal women, often in non-Western contexts, confront common assumptions regarding women's ritual experience and the emergence of subjectivity. This chapter will argue for an integration of insights from feminist Pentecostalism into the framework of doctrinal theology. I will explore the emergence of subjectivity in Pentecostal women in relation to the Holy Spirit, and will argue that a Pentecostal and feminist approach to pneumatology brings these critical elements together. My aim will be to foster a clearer vision of the intimate relation between the doctrine of God and the life of embodied community, thus showing that there is room within Christian doctrine for a richly textured exploration of the boundaries of subjectivity.

The Subject Is Dead

"The subject is dead," declares Eileen Schlee in the title of a classic paper.[1] The assertion is not all that surprising. In a landscape of poststructuralism, postmodernism and, for many, postfeminism, to harbor romantic notions about the emancipated subject is naïve at best. Of course, the dismantling of the subject is hardly the result of a lack of interest in subjectivity. Nick Mansfield observes in his anthology of subjectivity, "Rather than being triumphant because of the huge emphasis it now enjoys, the self is at risk; selfhood is seen to be in a state of perpetual crisis."[2] This may be observed in the many and varied interpretations of classic psychoanalysis. From Lacan and Beauvoir to Irigaray, we have been challenged to make claims concerning language's symbolic order and the reconceptualizing of subjectivity through the semiotic. Further, there is a sense—due largely to Foucault's influence—that any discussion of subjectivity must take into account the complex web of factors informing and shaping the embodied subject, as well as the fundamental role that power plays in personal formation.[3] Thus, whether entering the

1. Schlee, "The Subject Is Dead, Long Live the Female Subject," *Feminist Issues* 13, no. 2 (Fall 1993): 69–90.
2. Mansfield, *Subjectivity: Theories of the Self from Freud to Haraway* (New York: New York University Press, 2000), 2.
3. Though, as Mansfield argues, the ideal of the autonomous self-forming subject is almost ubiquitously dismissed and blamed on the classic scapegoat of the twentieth century: "the Enlightenment." See ibid., 13–24. Sarah Coakley, along with others, argues that this is an unfair reading. Instead, Coakley traces the development of the self throughout the Middle Ages. See

discussion of subjectivity from the perspective of gender theory or feminist theology, one is immediately met by a host of competing notions of the self. It is no wonder that the subject seems to be dead. For feminists, however, there is understandable hesitancy simply to move on from the subject. Mary McClintock Fulkerson notes that "we must not lose the subject. . . . We must change the subject."[4] For Schell, the importance of piecing together female subjectivity is grounded in its "history as a non-thing." So when she states that "the subject is dead," she also adds, "long live the feminine subject."[5]

But in what direction will future research on subjectivity turn? With subjectivity "at risk in the West,"[6] perhaps fresh paths may be discovered beyond complicated philosophical models of subjectivity, grounded instead in the experience of emerging subjects. In this connection, scholars have recently begun to explore the rich potential of feminist Pentecostal theology. This new voice in feminist studies poses challenges to gender studies and theology alike, with conclusions drawn from the experiences of Pentecostal women in non-Western contexts.

Sarojini Nadar asks us as to consider the experience of Christian women who are outside the World Council of Churches membership. Here she discovers that in some instances, Pentecostal women have emancipatory resources that mainline groups do not have.[7] Lene Sjørup argues for the primacy of Pentecostalism in establishing subjectivity in the lives of poor Chilean women. Moreover, she argues that it is precisely this subjectivity of

Sarah Coakley, "Visions of the Self in Late Medieval Christianity: Some Cross-Disciplinary Reflections," in *Powers and Submissions: Spirituality, Gender and Philosophy* (Oxford: Blackwell, 2002), 71–88.

4. Mary McClintock Fulkerson, *Changing the Subject: Women's Discourses and Feminist Theology* (Eugene, OR: Wipf and Stock, 2001), 11.

5. Schlee, "The Subject Is Dead, Long Live the Female Subject," 11.

6. Mansfield, *Subjectivity*, 2.

7. Sarojini Nadar, "On Being the Pentecostal Church," *Ecumenical Review* 56, no. 3 (2004): 366.

Pentecostal women (experienced from the inside out) that has the power to change wider social conditions.[8] Elsewhere, a joint research project links the embodied experience of ritual within Pentecostal communities in Salvador to the style of relation to self, others, and the wider social environment. Here women often become "important reference points in the neighbourhood, religious specialists who are frequently sought for guidance and healing."[9] In each of these instances, some form of personal subjectivity has occurred within the practice of Pentecostal communities. Evidently, the Pentecostal tradition has provided resources that many women would otherwise fail to have. Feminist literature is now beginning to report on these communities and to consider the broader theoretical implications.

This trend has coincided with a renewed awareness of the importance of pneumatology in the Christian doctrinal tradition. In recent decades, this has been evident in the work of scholars such as John Zizioulas, Wolfhart Pannenberg, and Robert Jenson. However, such theological projects have tended to ignore the challenging questions of gender and difference, to say nothing of the theological resources of Pentecostal studies. Drawing on the work of Andrea Hollingsworth, in what follows I will explore the potential of feminist Pentecostalism to inform Christian theological claims about subjectivity. I will argue that through an experience of the Holy Spirit—and the ensuing pneumatology—Pentecostal women are able to locate subjectivity within the economy of the Spirit and the incorporative life of God.

8. Lene Sjørup, "Pentecostals: The Power of the Powerless," *Dialog: A Journal of Theology* 41, no. 1 (2002): 25.
9. Miriam C. M. Rabelo, Sueli Ribeiro Mota, and Cláudio Roberto Almeida, "Cultivating the Senses and Giving In to the Sacred: Notes on Body and Experience among Pentecostal Women in Salvador, Brazil," *Journal of Contemporary Religion* 24, no. 1 (2009): 1–18.

Andrea Hollingsworth and the Divine Voice

In a 2009 *Pneuma* article on "Spirit and Voice," Andrea Hollingsworth contends that despite the uncommon pairing, feminism and Pentecostalism can forge a constructive collaboration around the shared values of "transformation, embodiment, and empowerment."[10] In noting the centrality of Spirit baptism, charismata, and witness, Hollingsworth shows that manifestations of the Spirit are often ecstatic, vocal, and communal.[11] She adds,

> [Due] to the centrality of the *charisms* of the Spirit in Pentecostalism and the widespread belief that they are given to men and women alike, ecstasy in the Spirit and expressiveness in worship are generally encouraged among Pentecostal women. In addition, women frequently act as ministers, healers, teachers, prophets, and preachers in their congregations. In light of the recent explosion of Pentecostal spirituality among women and men in the two-thirds world and the centrality of the Holy Spirit in Pentecostal faith, feminist theology's overall hesitancy to integrate ecstatic experiences of the Spirit with Spirit doctrine is definitely worth noting.[12]

Hollingsworth argues for the incorporation of Sarah Coakley's recent work on pneumatology in developing a feminist and Pentecostal approach to theology. By giving primacy to the place of prayer as a source for theology,[13] Coakley succeeds in "linking the Holy Spirit, Charismatic spirituality (especially vocal gifts of the Spirit), and women's empowerment."[14] For Hollingsworth, the manner in which Coakley appeals to divine empowerment through contemplation—as

---

10. Andrea Hollingsworth, "Spirit and Voice: Toward a Feminist Pentecostal Pneumatology," *Pneuma: The Journal of the Society for Pentecostal Studies* 29, no. 2 (2007): 190.
11. Ibid., 192.
12. Ibid., 193.
13. For an excellent example of how prayer is framed in Sarah Coakley's work, see Coakley, "Traditions of Spiritual Guidance: Dom John Chapman OSB (1865–1933) on the Meaning of 'Contemplation,'" in *Powers and Submissions*, 40–54.
14. Hollingsworth, "Spirit and Voice," 195.

CHRISTIAN DOCTRINE AND THE GRAMMAR OF DIFFERENCE

the manifestation of the Holy Spirit—provides a direct parallel with the charisms more typically related with Pentecostalism, such as glossolalia and prophecy.[15] Through this approach, Hollingsworth believes that an increased sense of subjectivity emerges in women, providing the ability to "give voice" in both the public and private spheres. In order to test these claims, Hollingsworth turns to Latina Pentecostal communities and, more specifically, to the experience of women experiencing the Holy Spirit within these communities. While she notes that there are many reasons to be skeptical about the benefits of Pentecostalism to Latin American communities—including the exploitation of faith for commercial gain and the profound entrenchment of patriarchal ideology—she points to the "substantial and growing body of sociological literature [that] points to the positive effects of Pentecostalism on the lives of Latin American women."[16] She cites field studies that show how conversion to Pentecostalism was more likely to see husbands give up their machismo, leading to far greater equality within the home.[17] Citing Elizabeth Brusco, Hollingsworth suggests that this in turn leads to an "increased sense of autonomy in wives."[18] Beyond the home, Pentecostal traditions have in many cases seen far greater numbers of women in leadership and ordained ministry than their mainline Protestant counterparts.[19] Hollingsworth's argument is that

15. There are certainly a range of other experiences in Pentecostal communities that bespeak empowerment. The relationship between physical encounter (e.g., the laying on of hands for gifts of healing) and subjectivity could also be explored through a similar lens. This chapter is primarily relating Hollingsworth work to the systematic fields, and for this reason will mainly consider the evocative language that Hollingsworth describes.

16. Hollingsworth, "Spirit and Voice," 188–99.

17. Lene Sjørup appeals to this "feminine ethos" (Brusco's term) to argue that in the case of Pentecostal conversion, there are clear expectations placed upon men to take greater responsibility within the home. The ensuing behaviour is thus interpreted in a manner more typically associated with the feminine. See Sjørup, "Pentecostals," 25. Rabelo, Mota, and Almeida argue that this same feminine ethos contributes to altering the power balance between spouses. Rabelo, Mota, and Almeida, "Cultivating the Senses and Giving In to the Sacred."

18. Hollingsworth, "Spirit and Voice," 199.

19. Ibid., 210 and 202.

it is embodied experiences of the Holy Spirit that have led to the empowerment of women within this tradition. She quotes Lene Sjørup, whose research showed that Chilean Pentecostal women felt empowered to effect social change through Spirit ecstasy. Sjørup notes, "Pentecostalism led to a new theology, where the believer became the subject of her own life."[20] Further, Hollingsworth observes that such experiences are often manifest in a vocal and public manner. R. Andrew Chestnut's research in Brazil found that women tend to experience these vocal gifts more often. Glossolalia is "speech for those whose tongue is tied by society, particularly for poor women of color."[21] With the addition of public prophecy, testimony, and hymnal participation, women in these communities are given space and opportunity to raise their voice and speak as subjects—perhaps for the first time. As Hollingsworth adds,

> Whether through *glossolalia*, preaching, prophesying, singing, or testifying, they are using their voices to articulate themselves powerfully and publicly, lead other congregants, develop an increased sense of agency/subjectivity, and find ways to cope with the suffering in their lives.[22]

Hollingsworth thus seeks to propose a constructive feminist Pentecostal pneumatology. She does this by suggesting that the Holy Spirit is the genesis of all voice, the voice that empowers or gives voice, the "condition and goal of all creaturely vocative efforts."[23] She draws from Scripture and from Christian tradition to demonstrate the prominence of the Spirit's role in giving voice—particularly the voice of life, justice, and empowerment. She also argues for the importance of utilizing as a category *voice*—which is relational and

---

20. Cited in ibid., 202.
21. R. Andrew Chestnut, *Born Again in Brazil: The Pentecostal Boom and the Pathogens of Poverty* (New Brunswick, NJ: Rutgers University Press, 1997).
22. Hollingsworth, "Spirit and Voice," 204.
23. Ibid., 205.

dynamic—instead of *word*. The dialectical nature of speaking and silence engages a Spirit who is not located "in one or the other interlocutor, but, rather, is mediated in and through the interlocutory process itself."[24] Thus by speaking of the Holy Spirit as "divine voice," Hollingsworth hopes to develop a pneumatology that encapsulates women's experience and "uphold[s] the feminist ideals of mutuality, plurality, embodiment as well as Pentecostal transformation, community, and ecstasy."[25]

Here, once more, I think the rhetorical pneumatology of Kevin Vanhoozer proves to be a valuable conversation partner. As has been seen, Vanhoozer argues that discourse between the Father, Son, and Spirit reveals God's being as a hospitable conversation.[26] As Vanhoozer builds on his rhetorical analogy more recently in *Remythologizing Theology*, he states, "God's presence is thus in the first instance personal, agential, and communicative rather than merely spatial, substantive, or metaphysical."[27] In this recent work, Vanhoozer fashions his rhetorical model around questions of fundamental doctrinal grammar, especially the divine-human relationship, and the transcendence and sovereignty of God. In his view, "Divine communication is ultimately oriented to communion, a divine-human fellowship that effects sanctification: the transformation of human communicants."[28] Similarly, Hollingsworth suggests that "giving voice and giving ear may be thought of as trinitarian practice, the creator's voice graciously opening us up to

---

24. Ibid., 207.
25. Ibid., 209.
26. Vanhoozer, "Theological Reflections on the Claim that God Speaks (Part 2)," in *Trinitarian Theology for the Church*, ed. Daniel J. Treier and David Lauber (Downers Grove, IL: InterVarsity, 2009), 50–78.
27. Vanhoozer, *Remythologizing Theology: Divine Action, Passion, and Authorship* (Cambridge: Cambridge University Press, 2010), 206.
28. Ibid., 494.

participating in the relationality of the eternally welcoming, evocative conversation of the Triune persons."[29]

These are potent themes, emerging directly from the doctrinal grammar of the Trinity. But contemporary Trinitarian theology generally pays no heed to the cry for emancipation found in feminist studies, nor to the embodied experience of people in Christian community. Nicola Slee argues that there is a direct correlation between the neglect of a fully worked-out pneumatology and the "repression and marginalisation of women themselves in Christian tradition."[30] Admittedly, Vanhoozer himself typifies a systematic approach in which pneumatology is presented in entirely theoretical categories, bearing little discernible consequence for embodied subjectivity. In his model, it is the (masculine) Logos who speaks, while the Spirit ensures that the listener actually hears and is affected.[31] Hollingsworth also notes the role of the Spirit is to bring wisdom to the silent, but she argues that there is a dialectical role to be played here: we are called both to listen and to speak. It is through both these actions that subjectivity emerges. In the final section of this chapter, I will suggest some ways in which Hollingsworth's work may speak to Vanhoozer's model, and I will draw some conclusions about the way a feminist Pentecostal pneumatology provides resources for both doctrinal reflection and feminist theology.

---

29. Hollingsworth, "Spirit and Voice," 208.
30. Nicola Slee, "The Holy Spirit and Spirituality," in *The Cambridge Companion to Feminist Theology*, ed. Susan Frank Parsons (Cambridge: Cambridge University Press, 2002), 172.
31. Though Vanhoozer does note that 'the Spirit makes public an inner-trinitarian conversation'." See Vanhoozer, "Theological Reflections on the Claim that God Speaks (Part 2)," 52.

Subject to Spirit:
The Promise of Pentecostal Feminist Pneumatology

From the perspective of creaturely difference, there are several instructive facets of Hollingsworth's model. She has placed her model entirely within the context of embodied community. By contrast, though Vanhoozer makes reference to the church, these comments only vaguely point to the communication of "salvation" and eschatological hope.[32] Indeed, the same charge could be laid against Coakley, whose appeals to transformative spiritual practices nearly always give the impression of an isolated self. Although Coakley hints at inner empowerment, the actual encounter with the Spirit in no way manifests the kind of public identity that one finds in Hollingsworth's model. Coakley and Vanhoozer both argue for the efficacy of the Spirit, and Coakley suggests that this will affect the community. Yet it is only in the Pentecostal approach that there is any concrete example of public empowerment. The way non-Western Pentecostal scholars routinely provide examples of such public identity from fieldwork highlights the tendency to overlook real communities in academic theorising.

Further, in Hollingsworth we find that the work of the Holy Spirit is given sociopolitical context and direction. While Vanhoozer's "pathos" speaks of a work of rational transformation, Hollingsworth argues that the Spirit speaks life, justice, and empowerment.[33] She notes,

> The Spirit's strengthening power was especially important for Hildegard as a woman. Her context was a crushing, patriarchal society that often suppressed female voices from any kind of public area. But for

---

32. Ibid., 57–58.

33. Hollingsworth, "Spirit and Voice," 205–6. In contrast, Vanhoozer states, "The 'pathos effect' is the Spirit's persuading the reader to embrace the point of view expressed in the Logos." Vanhoozer, "Theological Reflections on the Claim that God Speaks (Part 2)," 63.

Hildegard, the intense experiences of the Holy Spirit in mystical and ecstatic prayer was the source of the courage that enabled her to fulfil her prophetic call, even in a context that had conditioned her to view herself with some disdain simply because she was a female.[34]

Notably, Nicola Slee also argues that matters of justice, empowerment, and relational connectedness are hallmarks of feminist spiritualty.[35] Yet while studies of feminist spirituality are relatively common, it is necessary also to take the next step—as Hollingsworth herself does—by drawing questions of spiritual practice and emancipation into a broader doctrinal (in this instance, pneumatological) framework. For feminist theology, it is precisely a doctrine of the Holy Spirit that is able to encompass these diverse dimensions of experience and embodiment, and to articulate their underlying Christian grammar.

The dialectic interplay described by Hollingsworth gives expression to the place of difference within Pentecostal communities. She writes, "Since it is mediated through a vast variety of human voices, the Spirit's voice is astonishingly polyvocal."[36] The divine voice does not denote gender, and is bound neither to the role of speaker nor listener. Difference is not only welcome but necessary in this account of the Spirit. For example, such an approach could easily be applied to Mary McClintock Fulkerson's call for radical textualization.[37] Certainly it is noteworthy that both models rely on vocal categories to denote the divine and also the interaction of humanity with God. Questions remain regarding those for whom normative vocal categories are unavailable. Perhaps, however, the categories of voice, speaking, and hearing are more nuanced than a simple example of human-to-human vocal conversation. At any rate,

34. Hollingsworth, "Spirit and Voice," 206.
35. Slee, "The Holy Spirit and Spirituality," 179–82.
36. Hollingsworth, "Spirit and Voice,"
37. Fulkerson, *Changing the Subject.*

constructing a model not around Logos but pathos, the Spirit, presses the divine–human interaction beyond the bounds of language and reason.

In Hollingsworth's model there is also an emphasis on voice, and the wider body of reflection on Pentecostal pneumatology provides opportunities to reconsider the boundaries of language within the context of glossolalia. While tongues-speech is often associated in Pentecostal circles as a sign of fully entering into the tradition, it is also a spiritual act that challenges Western notions of God, religious experience, and epistemology.[38] James K. A. Smith has written an insightful essay on tongues-speech in which he suggests that we might speak of glossolalia as resistance discourse. In spite of philosophy giving little attention to this "strange, quite extraordinary" language, Smith argues that the apparent limits of tongues-speech when applied to philosophy are precisely what make it most interesting.[39] Tongues-speech resists the categories of philosophical analysis and thus "one might say that such a prayer is a kind of sacramental practice of emptying, recognising the failure of even language to even measure up to such an exchange. Glossolalic prayer is a means of making oneself both receptive to and a conduit of the Spirit's work."[40] Smith, however, wants to draw from social and ethical philosophy also to demonstrate the resistive nature of glossolalia. Using speech–act theory to describe glossolalia as an act of performance, Smith argues,

> As an *action*, one of the things that speaking in tongues *does* is to effect a kind of social resistance to the powers-that-be. Or perhaps we should say that tongues-speech is the language of faith communities which are

38. Rabelo, Mota, and Almeida, "Cultivating the Senses and Giving In to the Sacred," 2.
39. James K. A. Smith, "Tongues as a Resistant Discourse: A Philosophical Perspective," in *Speaking in Tongues: Multi-Disciplinary Perspectives*, ed. Mark Cartledge (Carlisle, UK: Paternoster, 2002), 81.
40. Ibid., 84.

marginalised by the powers-that-be, and such speech is indicative of a kind of eschatological resistance of the powers. We might say that the proletariat speaks in tongues.[41]

Smith applies this case of resistance to the capitalist market, and suggestively points to the decrease in glossolalia within American Assemblies of God congregations when they climb "the ladder of social class."[42] The case could also be made here for the role of glossolalia in women's subjectivity. The accusations of patriarchy made against language itself—particularly by Irigaray—have been felt profoundly by all strains of feminism. When appeals are made to the word, or acts of speech, the critique of language lurks in the shadows, ready to dismantle every constructive effort. Yet glossolalia does something with language that defies the rules and transgresses the boundaries—as one might expect if this is indeed the work of the Spirit, of God without boundaries.

Finally, in drawing subjectivity and the doctrine of the Holy Spirit together, something must be said of the eschatological. As the Spirit calls us and empowers us, likewise the Spirit leads us to the ends of ourselves. The emerging subject is drawn into the ultimate reality of the eschaton. Here we may find a creative tension through which subjectivity itself may be transgressed. Ontological categories of personhood are transformed for those who are "in" the Spirit. Typically, when spirituality is discussed there are at least implicit overtones of self-surrender and abandonment. By contrast, Rowan Williams gives an account of subjectivity *in via*, defending the importance of the subject before God. Unless we are at home in our created "selves" we cannot grow into the image of God.[43] Williams

---

41. Ibid., 87.
42. Ibid., 110.
43. Rowan Williams, "Sapientia and the Trinity: Reflections on De Trinitate," in *Collectanea Augustiniana: Mélanges T. J. van Bavel*, ed. Bernard Bruning et al. (Leuven: Leuven University Press, 1990), 321.

CHRISTIAN DOCTRINE AND THE GRAMMAR OF DIFFERENCE

wants to affirm personal subjectivity as part of God's creative and redemptive economy. Subjectivity itself is part of the divine invitation, a call to the other. He writes,

> To redefine the problem in terms of sheer identity is to say that peace, unity, reconciliation, even love, are really masks of the absence of difference: all identity must be reduced to the eternal sameness of divine act. But the trinitarian pattern tells us that the divine act is not an eternal sameness at all, but relational act; so that the challenge for creatures is not the abolition of difference and the cancellation of the subject, but the subject's growth into precisely the recognition of and enactment of the self's reality *in* the other that is in the heart of the theological vision.[44]

Williams points here to a conception of the Godhead that itself transgresses the boundaries of subjectivity. Contemporary theologians argue passionately for the subjectivity of God, as opposed to objectifying the Trinity. This, however, might turn out to be a false dichotomy. Elsewhere, speaking of the divine persons, Williams notes, "The whole language of self is unhelpful here, I suspect, though I realise I have been using it. We are at a loss to find useful ways of talking about life characterised by activity that is more like intelligent activity than any other, yet is neither the life of a single subject, not the history of several individual subjects."[45] Instead, Williams uses John of the Cross to describe the life of the Godhead as the going out from self-identity into the other, a divine speaking that brings forth an ever-wider pattern of relational involvement.[46] The divine discourse is not a unilateral address, but an invitation that enables participation. And just as glossolalia defies ordinary rules of speech, the ongoing Triune conversation transgresses the boundaries

44. Williams, "The Deflections of Desire: Negative Theology in Trinitarian Disclosure," in *Silence and the Word: Negative Theology and Incarnation*, ed. Oliver Davies and Denys Turner (Cambridge: Cambridge University Press, 2002), 131.
45. Williams, "What Does Love Know? St Thomas on the Trinity," *New Blackfriars* 82, no. 964 (June 2001): 260–72.
46. Williams "The Deflections of Desire," 118.

of speech and subjectivity. If there is a subjectivity of the Triune persons, then these persons must also be thought of as transgressing "each other" in love and desire, gently breaking the bounds of subjectivity. The divine life is a pattern of "gift and reception so radical that we have not finally suitable categories. . . . [We are faced] with a plain lack of adequate categories for speaking about something like subjectivity that cannot be accounted for in the terms of our standard discourse of sameness and otherness, subjects and object."[47] Only in light of this doctrine—a doctrine of the Trinity—can we understand the Spirit who brings us into the life of the Godhead and into the binary-dissolving reflexivity of divine discourse.

A Teleology of the Subject?

Despite the ways in which contemporary theorists open up discourse around subjectivity, within a Christian systematic theology the subject always and only ever subsists insofar as it is located in the movement of the divine economy. The subject is sustained by, drawn into, and lovingly transgressed by the Triune life. Here we have a picture of subjectivity being recast eschatologically. The created subject must not be lost; it is affirmed; it is necessary. Its emergence is the work of the Spirit. However, subjectivity is not the last word either, and each subject is invited to take up a part in the transgressive discourse of the Triune God. It is within the divine life that we discover that subjectivity is not autonomous or self-contained; the self's autonomy is lovingly transgressed as it is opened to participate in a divine discourse that is inexhaustibly full and free. Paradoxically, such transgression of subjectivity is possible only for those who are at

47. Ibid., 122.

home in their created selves. Only as we learn to be creatures do we become subject to Spirit.

Bibliography

Abraham, Susan. "Strategic Essentialism in Nationalist Discourses: Sketching a Feminist Agenda in the Study of Religion." *Journal of Feminist Studies in Religion* 25, no. 1 (Spring) (2009): 156–61.

Albrecht, Gloria H. "Unmasking the Differences: Nonviolence and Social Control." *Cross Currents* 52, no. 1 (2002): 16–27.

Alcoff, Linda. "Cultural Feminism versus Post-Structuralism: The Identity Crisis in Feminist Theory." *Signs: Journal of Women, Culture and Society* 13, no. 3 (Spring 1988): 405–36.

Alston, William P. "Religious Language." In *The Oxford Handbook of Philosophy of Religion*, edited by William J. Wainwright, 220–44. Oxford: Oxford University Press, 2005.

Armour, Ellen T. *Deconstruction: Feminist Theology and the Problem of Difference.* Chicago: University of Chicago Press, 1999.

Augustine. *Confessions.* Translated by Maria Boulding. The Works of Saint Augustine: A Translation for the 21st Century, edited by John E. Rotelle. New York: New City, 1997.

———. *On Genesis: A Refutation of the Manichees, Unfinished Literal Commentary on Genesis, the Literal Meaning of Genesis.* Translated by Edmund Hill and Matthew O'Connell. The Works of Saint Augustine: A Translation for the 21st Century, edited by John E. Rotelle. New York: New City, 2002.

Ávila, Teresa of. *The Interior Castle: Study Edition*. Edited and translated by Kieran Kavanaugh and Otilo Rodriguez. Washington, DC: ICS, 2010.

———.*The Book of my Life*. Translated by Mirabia Starr. Boston: New Seeds Books, 2007.

Ayres, Lewis. "On the Practice and Teaching of Christian Doctrine." *Gregorianum* 80 (1999): 33–94.

Bailey, Randall C., Tat-siong Benny Liew, and Fernando F. Segovia. *They Were All Together in One Place? Toward Minority Biblical Criticism*. Society of Biblical Literature Semeia Studies. Atlanta: Society of Biblical Literature, 2009.

Bailey, Scott. Review of *On What Cannot Be Said: Apophatic Discourses in Philosophy, Religion, Literature, and the Arts*, by William Franke. *Christianity & Literature* 59, no. 2 (2010): 373–81.

Barth, Karl. *Church Dogmatics*. Edited by G. W. Bromley and T. F. Torrance. Translated by J. W. Edwards, et al. Vol. IV.I. Peabody, MA: Hendrickson, 2010.

Basinger, David. "Practical Implications." In *The Openness of God: A Biblical Challenge to the Traditional Understanding of God*, edited by Clark H. Pinnock, et al., 155–76. Downers Grove, IL: InterVarsity, 1994.

Bauman, Whitney. *Theology, Creation and Environmental Ethics: From Creatio Ex Nihilo to Terra Nullius*. Routledge Studies in Religion. New York: Routledge, 2009.

Beattie, Tina. *God's Mother, Eve's Advocate: A Marian Narrative of Women's Salvation*. London: Continuum, 2002.

Beauvoir, Simone de. *The Second Sex*. Translated by Constance Borde and Sheila Malovany-Chevallier. New York: Alfred A. Knopf, 2010.

Bernauer, James, and Jeremy Carrette. "Introduction: The Enduring Problem: Foucault, Theology and Culture." In *Michel Foucault and Theology: The Politics of Religious Experience*, edited by James Bernauer and Jeremy Carrette, 1–16. Aldershot: Ashgate, 2004.

Bieler, Andrea, and David Plüss. "In This Moment of Utter Vulnerability: Tracing Gender in Presiding." In *Presiding Like a Woman*, edited by Nicola Slee and Stephen Burns, 112–22. London: SPCK, 2010.

Boff, Leonardo. *Holy Trinity, Perfect Community*. Translated by Phillip Berryman. Maryknoll, NY: Orbis, 2000.

———. *The Maternal Face of God: The Feminine and Its Religious Experience*. Translated by Robert R. Barr and John W. Dierksmeire. San Francisco: Harper and Row, 1987.

———. *Trinity and Society*. Translated by Paul Burns. Maryknoll, NY: Orbis, 1988.

———. *When Theology Listens to the Poor*. Translated by Robert R. Barr. San Francisco: Harper and Row, 1988.

Boulding, Maria. "Introduction." In Augustine, *Confessions*. The Works of Saint Augustine: A Translation for the 21st Century, edited by John E. Rotelle. New York: New City, 2007.

Braidotti, Rosi. *Nomadic Subjects: Embodiment and Sexual Differences in Contemporary Feminist Theory*. New York: Columbia University Press, 1994.

———. *Patterns of Dissonance: A Study of Women in Contemporary Philosophy*. Translated by Elizabeth Guild. New York: Routledge, 1991.

Briggs, Sheila. "The Politics of Identity and the Politics of Interpretation." *Union Seminary Quarterly Review* 43 (1989): 169–70.

Brooks, Ann. *Post Feminism: Feminism, Cultural Theory and Cultural Forms*. London: Routledge, 1997.

Butler, Judith. *Bodies That Matter: On the Discursive Limits of "Sex."* New York: Routledge, 1993.

———. *Gender Trouble: Feminism and the Subversion of Identity*. 2nd ed. New York Routledge, 2008.

———. *Giving an Account of Oneself*. New York: Fordham University Press, 2005.

———. *Undoing Gender.* New York: Routledge, 2004.

Butterworth, Molly, and Lisa M. Diamond. "Questioning Gender and Sexual Identity: Dynamic Links over Time." *Sex Roles* 59 (2008): 356–76.

Byatt, A. S. *Possession.* London: Vintage, 2009.

Cady, Linell Elizabeth. "Identity, Feminist Theory, and Theology." In *Horizons in Feminist Theology: Identity, Tradition, and Norms,* edited by Rebecca S. Chopp and Sheila Greeve Davaney, 17–32. Minneapolis: Fortress Press, 1997.

Caputo, John. "Madness, Hermeneutics and the Night of Truth." In *Michel Foucault and Theology: The Politics of Religious Experience,* edited by James Bernauer and Jeremy Carrette, 117–39. Aldershot: Ashgate, 2004.

Carr, Anne E. *Transforming Grace: Christian Tradition and Women's Experience.* San Francisco: Harper & Row, 1988.

Carrette, Jeremy R. *Foucault and Religion: Spiritual Corporality and Political Spirituality.* New York: Routledge, 2000.

Cavanaugh, William T. "The City: Beyond Secular Parodies." In *Radical Orthodoxy: A New Theology,* edited by John Milbank, Catherine Pickstock, and Graham Ward, 182–200. New York: Routledge, 1998.

Chestnut, R. Andrew. *Born Again in Brazil: The Pentecostal Boom and the Pathogens of Poverty.* New Jersey: Rutgers University Press, 1997.

Chopp, Rebecca S. "Anointed to Preach: Speaking of Sin in the Midst of Grace." In *The Portion of the Poor: Good News to the Poor in the Wesleyan Tradition.* edited by M. Douglas Meeks, 97–111. Nashville: Abingdon, 1994.

———. *The Power to Speak: Feminism, Language, God.* New York: Crossroad, 1989.

Chopp, Rebecca S., and Sheila Davaney. *Horizons in Feminist Theology: Identity, Tradition, and Norms.* Minneapolis: Fortress Press, 1997.

Clark, Elizabeth. "Augustine on Marriage." In *Feminism and Theology*, edited by Janet Martin Soskice and Diana Lupton. Oxford: Oxford University Press, 2003.

Clark, Mary T. *Augustine*. Outstanding Christian Thinkers, edited by Brian Davies. Continuum: New York, 1994.

Coakley, Sarah. "Analytic Philosophy of Religion in Feminist Perspective: Some Questions." In *Powers and Submissions: Spirituality, Gender and Philosophy*, 98–106. Oxford: Blackwell, 2002.

———. "Contemporary Religious Epistemology: The Turn to 'Femininity.'" In *Analytic Theology: New Essays in the Philosophy of Religion*, edited by Oliver D. Crisp and Michael C. Rea, 284–312. Oxford: Oxford University Press, 2009

———. "Feminist Theology." In *Modern Christian Thought*, Vol. 2, *The Twentieth Century*, edited by James C. Livingston, et al. Minneapolis: Fortress Press, 2006.

———. "Gender and Knowledge in Modern Western Philosophy: The 'Man of Reason' and the 'Feminine' 'Other' in Enlightenment and Romantic Thought." In *Powers and Submissions: Spirituality, Gender and Philosophy*, 89–97. Oxford: Blackwell, 2002.

———. "Is There a Future for Gender and Theology? On Gender, Contemplation, and the Systematic Task." *Criterion* 47, no. 1 (2009): 2–12.

———. "Kenosis: Theological Meanings and Gender Connotations." In *The Work of Love*, edited by John Polkinghorne, 192–210. Grand Rapids: Eerdmans, 2001.

———. "'Persons' in the 'Social' Doctrine of the Trinity: Current Analytic Discussion and 'Cappadocian' Theology." In *Powers and Submissions: Spirituality, Philosophy and Gender*, 109–29. Oxford: Blackwell, 2002.

———. "Persons in the Social Doctrine of the Trinity: A Critique of Current Analytic Discussion." In *The Incarnation: An Interdisciplinary Symposium on the Incarnation of the Son of God*, edited by Stephen T. Davis, et al., 146–63. Oxford: Oxford University Press, 2002.

———. *Powers and Submissions: Spirituality, Philosophy and Gender*. Challenges in Contemporary Theology. Oxford: Blackwell, 2002.

———. "Prologue: Powers and Submissions." In *Powers and Submissions: Spirituality, Philosophy and Gender*, xii–xx. Oxford: Blackwell, 2002.

———. Review of *Sexing the Trinity: Gender, Culture and the Divine*, by Gavin D'Costa. *Theology & Sexuality: The Journal of the Institute for the Study of Christianity & Sexuality* 11, no. 3 (2005): 91–94.

———. "Traditions of Spiritual Guidance: Dom John Chapman OSB (1865–1933) on the Meaning of 'Contemplation.'" In *Powers and Submissions: Spirituality, Gender and Philosophy*, 40–54. Oxford: Blackwell, 2002.

———. "Visions of the Self in Late Medieval Christianity: Some Cross-Disciplinary Reflections." In *Powers and Submissions: Spirituality, Gender and Philosophy*, 71–88. Oxford: Blackwell, 2002.

———. "Why Three? Some Further Reflections on the Origins on the Doctrine of the Trinity." In *The Making and Remaking of Christian Doctrine: Essays in Honour of Maurice Wiles*, edited by Maurice F. Wiles, Sarah Coakley and David A. Pailin, 29–56. Oxford: Oxford University Press, 1993.

———. "The Woman at the Altar: Cosmological Disturbance of Gender Subversion?" *Anglican Theological Review* 86, no. 1 (2004): 75–93.

Code, Lorraine. "Taking Subjectivity into Account." In *Feminist Epistemologies*, edited by Linda Alcoff and Elizabeth Potter, 15–48. Thinking Gender. New York: Routledge, Chapman and Hall, 1993.

Crisp, Oliver. "Karl Barth on Creation." In *Karl Barth and Evangelical Theology*, edited by Sung Wook Chung, 77–95. Grand Rapids: Baker Academic, 2006.

D'Costa, Gavin. *Sexing the Trinity: Gender, Culture and the Divine*. London: SCM, 2000.

DaCosta, Jacqueline. "Can Apophatic Theology Be Applied to Goddessing as Well as to God?" *Feminist Theology: The Journal of the Britain & Ireland School of Feminist Theology* 11, no. 1 (2002): 82–98.

Dallavale, Nancy. "Neither Idolatry nor Iconoclasm: A Critical Essentialism for Catholic Feminist Theology." *Horizons* 25, no. 1 (1998): 23–42.

Daly, Mary. *Beyond God the Father: Toward a Philosophy of Women's Liberation*. Boston: Beacon, 1973.

Davis, Colin. *After Poststructuralism: Reading, Stories, Theory*. London: Routledge, 2004.

DeHart, Paul J. *The Trial of the Witnesses: The Rise and Decline of Postliberal Theology* Challenges in Contemporary Theology, edited by Gareth Jones and Lewis Ayres. Blackwell: Oxford, 2006.

Derrida, Jacques. *Dissemination*. Translated by Barbara Johnson. London: Althone, 1981.

Deveaux, Monique. "Feminism and Empowerment: A Critical Reading of Foucault." In *Feminist Interpretations of Michel Foucault*, edited by Susan J. Hekman, 211–39. University Park, PA: Pennsylvania University Press, 1996.

DiNoia, J. A. Review of *God for Us*, by Catherine Mowry LaCugna. *Modern Theology* 9 (1993): 215–16.

Dreyfus, Hubert, and Paul Rabinow. *Michel Foucault: Beyond Structuralism and Hermeneutics*. 2nd ed. Chicago: University of Chicago Press, 1983.

Drolet, Michael. "Introduction " In *The Postmodernism Reader: Foundational Texts*, edited by Michael Drolet, 1–35. New York: Routledge, 2004.

Edgardh, Ninna. "Difference and Desire—a Queer Reading." *Dialog: A Journal of Theology* 48, no. 1 (2009): 42–48.

Eisenstein, Zillah. *The Radical Future of Liberal Feminism*. New York: Longman, 1981.

Elbow, Peter. "The Uses of Binary Thinking " *Journal of Advanced Composition* 13, no. 1 (1993): 51–78.

Engel, Mary Potter. "Evil, Sin, and Violation of the Vulnerable." In *Lift Every Voice: Constructing Christian Theologies from the Underside*, edited by Susan Brooks Thistlewaite and Mary Potter Engel, 152–64. San Francisco: Harper San Francisco, 1990.

English, Leona M. "Revisiting Voice, Subjectivity and Circles: Feminist Pedagogy in the Twenty-First Century." *Journal of Adult Theological Education* 5, no. 2 (2008): 112–25.

Ernst-Habib, Margit. ""Chosen by Grace': Reconsidering the Doctrine of Predestination." In *Feminist and Womanist Essays in Reformed Dogmatics*, edited by Amy Plantinga Pauw and Serene Jones, 75–94. Louisville: Westminster John Knox, 2006.

Faludi, Susan. *Backlash: The Undeclared War against Women.* Crown, 1991.

Foucault, Michel. *The Hermeneutics of the Subject: Lectures at the Collège de France 1981–1982.* Edited by Frédéric Gros. New York: Picador, 2001.

———. "Interview with Raymond Bellours." In *Aesthetics, Method, and Epistemology*, edited by James D. Faubion. London: Penguin, 1998.

———. *The Order of Things: An Archaeology of the Human Sciences.* A translation of *Les Mots et le Choses.* New York: Vintage, 1994.

———. *Power/Knowledge: Selected Interviews and Other Writings, 1972–1977.* Edited by Colin Gordon. Translated by Colin Gordon, et al. New York: Pantheon, 1980.

———. "Technologies of the Self." In *Technologies of the Self: A Seminar with Michel Foucault*, edited by Luther H. Martin, et al., 16–49. Cambridge: The University of Massachusetts Press, 1988.

———. *The Use of Pleasure.* Translated by Robert Hurley. Vol. 2, *The History of Sexuality.* London: Penguin, 1992.

———. *The Will to Knowledge.* Translated by Robert Hurley. Vol. 1, *The History of Sexuality.* New York: Penguin, 1981.

Fox-Genovese, Elizabeth. *Feminism Is Not the Story of My Life*. New York: Anchor, 1996.

Franke, William. *On What Cannot Be Said: Apophatic Discourses in Philosophy, Religion, Literature, and the Arts*. 2 vols. Notre Dame: University of Notre Dame Press, 2007.

Fredriksen, Paula. *Sin: The Early History of an Idea*. Princeton: Princeton University Press, 2012.

Friedan, Betty. *The Feminist Mystique*. New York: W. W. Norton and Co., 1963.

Fulkerson, Mary McClintock. *Changing the Subject: Women's Discourses and Feminist Theology*. Eugene, OR: Wipf and Stock, 2001.

———. "Feminist Theology." In *The Cambridge Companion to Postmodern Theology*, edited by Kevin J. Vanhoozer, 109–25. Cambridge: Cambridge University Press, 2003.

Fuss, Diana. "'Essentially Speaking': Luce Irirgary's Language of Essence." *Hypatia* 3 (Winter 1989): 62–80.

———. *Essentially Speaking: Feminism, Nature and Difference*. New York: Routledge, 1989.

Gonzalez, Michelle A. *Created in God's Image: An Introduction to Feminist Theological Anthropology*. Maryknoll, NY: Orbis, 2007.

Grenz, Stanley J. *Rediscovering the Triune God: The Trinity in Contemporary Theology*. Minneapolis: Fortress Press, 2004.

———. *The Social God and the Relational Self*. The Matrix of Christian Theology. Louisville: Westminster John Knox, 2001.

Griffin, David R. "A Process Theology of Creation." *Mid-Stream* 1–2, (Fall–Winter 1973): 48–70.

Grope, Elizabeth. "Creation Ex Nihilo and Ex Amore: Ontological Freedom in the Theologies of John Zizioulas and Catherine Mowry LaCugna." *Modern Theology* 21, no. 3 (2005): 463–96.

Gunton, Colin E. *The Promise of Trinitarian Theology*. Edinburgh: T & T Clark, 1991.

Halkes, Catharina J. M. *New Creation: Christian Feminism and the Renewal of the Earth*. London: SPCK, 1991.

Hampson, Daphne. *Theology and Feminism*. Signposts in Theology. Oxford: Basil Blackwell, 1990.

Hart, David Bentley. *The Beauty of the Infinite: The Aesthetics of Christian Truth*. Grand Rapids: Eerdmans, 2003.

Hartsock, Nancy. "Foucault on Power: A Theory for Women?" In *Feminism/Postmodernism*, edited by Linda J. Nicholson, 157–75. New York: Routledge, 1990.

Hasker, William. "A Philosophical Perspective." In *The Openness of God: A Biblical Challenge to the Traditional Understanding of God*, edited by Clark H. Pinnock, et al., 126–54. Downers Grove, IL: InterVarsity, 1994.

Hoffman, E. *Lost in Translation*. London: Minerva, 1991.

Hollingsworth, Andrea. "Spirit and Voice: Toward a Feminist Pentecostal Pneumatology." *Pneuma: The Journal of the Society for Pentecostal Studies* 29, no. 2 (2007): 189–213.

Honneth, Axel. *The Critique of Power: Reflective Stages in Critical Social Theory*. Translated by Kenneth Baynes. Cambridge: The MIT Press, 1993.

Hütter, Reinhard. "(Re-)Forming Freedom: Reflections 'After Veritas Splendour' on Freedom's Fate in Modernity and Protestantism's Antinomian Captivity." *Modern Theology* 17, no. 2 (2001): 117–61.

Infinito, Justin. "Ethical Self-Formation: A Look at the Later Foucault." *Educational Theory* 53, no. 2 (2003): 155–71.

Ingraffa, Brian. *Postmodern Theory and Biblical Theology*. Cambridge: Cambridge University Press, 1995.

Irigaray, Luce. "Equal to Whom." In *The Postmodern God*, edited by Graham Ward. Oxford: Blackwell, 1997.

———. *An Ethics of Sexual Difference*. Translated by Carolyn Burke and Gillian C. Gill. London: Continuum, 2004.

———. *The Sex Which Is Not One*. Translated by Catherine Porter and Carolyn Burke. Ithaca, NY: Cornell University Press, 1985.

———. *Thinking the Difference: For a Peaceful Revolution*. New York: Routledge 1994.

———. "Women-Amongst-Themselves: Creating a Woman-to-Woman Sociality." In *The Irigaray Reader*, edited by Margaret Whitford, 190–97. Oxford: Blackwell, 1991.

Isasi-Díaz, Ada María. *Mujerista Theology: A Theology for the 21st Century*. Maryknoll, NY: Orbis, 1996.

Isherwood, L., and D. McEwan. *Introducing Feminist Theology*. 2nd ed. Sheffield: Sheffield Academic, 2001.

Jantzen, Grace. "Becoming Divine: Toward a Feminist Philosophy of Religion." Bloomington: Indiana University Press, 1999.

———. "Power, Gender, and Christian Mysticism." Cambridge: Cambridge University Press, 1995.

Jenson, Robert W. "Creation as a Triune Act." *Word and World* 2, no. 1 (Winter 1982): 34–43.

———. "The Father, He . . ." In *Speaking the Christian God: The Holy Trinity and the Challenge of Feminism*, edited by Alvin F. Kimmel Jr., 95–119. Grand Rapids: Eerdmans, 1992.

Johnson, Elizabeth A. *She Who Is: The Mystery of God in Feminist Theological Discourse*. 10th anniversary ed. New York: Crossroad, 1992.

Jones, Serene. *Feminist Theory and Christian Theology: Cartographies of Grace*. Guides to Theological Inquiry. Minneapolis: Fortress Press, 2000.

Julian of Norwich. *Showings*. Translated by Edmund Colledge and James Walsh. Classics of Western Spirituality. New York: Paulist, 1978.

Kamitsuka, Margaret D. *Feminist Theology and the Challenge of Difference*. AAR Reflection and Theory in the Study of Religion Series, edited by James Wetzel. Oxford: Oxford University Press, 2007.

———. "Toward a Feminist and Postmodern and Postcolonial Interpretation of Sin." *Journal of Religion* 84, no. 2 (2004): 179–211.

Karras, Valerie A. "Eschatology." In *The Cambridge Companion to Feminist Theology*, edited by Susan Frank Parsons, 243–60. Cambridge: Cambridge University Press, 2002.

Keen, Craig. "Holy, Holy, Holy: The World Need Not Have Been" In *The Transgression of the Integrity of God*, edited by Thomas J. Bridges and Nathan R. Kerr, 103–22. Eugene, OR: Cascade, 2012.

Keller, Catherine. *Face of the Deep: A Theology of Becoming*. Abingdon: Routledge, 2003.

———. *From a Broken Web: Sexism, Separation and the Self*. Boston: Beacon, 1986.

———. *God and Power: Counter-Apocalyptic Journeys*. Minneapolis: Fortress Press, 2005.

———. "Power Lines." *Theology Today* 52, no. 2 (1995): 188–203.

———. "Process and Chaosmos: The Whiteheadean Fold in the Discourse of Difference." In *Process and Difference: Between Cosmological and Poststructuralist Postmodernisms*, edited by Catherine Keller and Anne Daniell, 55–72. Albany: State University of New York, 2002.

Kelsey, David. *Eccentric Existence: A Theological Anthropology*. 2 vols. Louisville: Westminster John Knox, 2009.

Kim, C. W. Maggie, Susan M. St. Ville, and Susan M. Simonaitis. *Transfigurations: Theology and the French Feminists*. Minneapolis: Fortress Press, 1993.

Kotzé, Annamaré. "The 'Anti-Manichaean' Passage in *Confessions* 3 and Its 'Manichaean Audience.'" *Vigiliae Christianae* 62 (2008): 187–200.

Kristeva, Julia. *Powers and Horrors: An Essay on Abjection*. New York: Columbia University Press, 1982.

Küng, Hans. *Women in Christianity*. Translated by John Bowden. New York: Continuum, 2001.

LaCugna, Catherine Mowry. *God for Us*. New York: Harper Collins, 1991.

———. "The Practical Trinity." *Christian Century* 109, no. 22 (July 1992): 15–22.

Laird, Martin. "The "Open Country Whose Name Is Prayer": Apophasis, Deconstruction, and Contemplative Practice." *Modern Theology* 21, no. 1 (2005): 141–55.

Liew, Tat-siong Benny. *What Is Asian American Biblical Hermeneutics? Reading the New Testament*. Intersections: Asian and Pacific American Transcultural Studies. Honolulu: University of Hawaii Press, 2008.

Lindbeck, George. *The Church in the Postliberal Age*. Edited by James J. Buckley. Radical Traditions. London: SCM, 2002.

Lloyd, Genevieve. *The Man of Reason: "Male" and "Female" in Western Philosophy*. London: Routledge, 1984.

Lloyd, G. E. R. "Polarity and Analogy: Two Types of Argumentation in Early Greek Thought." Cambridge: Cambridge University Press, 1966.

Loades, Ann. *Feminist Theology: A Reader*. London: SPCK, 1990.

Mansfield, Nick. *Subjectivity: Theories of the Self from Freud to Haraway*. New York: New York University Press, 2000.

Matthews, Eric. *Twentieth-Century French Philosophy*. Oxford: Oxford University Press, 1996.

McCabe, Herbert. *The New Creation*. 3rd ed. London: Continuum, 2010.

McDougall, Joy Ann. "Keeping Feminist Faith with Christian Traditions: A Look at Christian Feminist Theology Today." *Modern Theology* 24, no. 1 (January 2008): 103–24.

———. "Sin—No More? A Feminist Re-Visioning of a Christian Theology of Sin." *Anglican Theological Review* 88, no. 2 (2006): 215–35.

McFague, Sallie. *Models of God: Theology for an Ecological, Nuclear Age*. Philadelphia: Fortress Press, 1987.

———. *The Body of God: An Ecological Theology* Minneapolis: Fortress Press, 1993.

McLaren, Margaret A. "Foucault and Feminism: Power, Resistance, Freedom." In *Feminism and the Final Foucault*, edited by Dianna Taylor and Karen Vintges, 214–43. Urbana, IL: University of Illinois Press, 2004.

McWhorter, Ladelle. "Practicing Practicing." In *Feminism and the Final Foucault*, edited by Dianna Taylor and Karen Vintges, 143–62. Urbana, IL: University of Illinois Press, 2004.

Merchant, Carolyn. *The Death of Nature: Women, Ecology, and the Scientific Revolution*. San Francisco: Harper Collins, 1980.

Milem, Bruce. Review of *On What Cannot Be Said: Apophatic Discourses in Philosophy, Religion, Literature and the Arts*, by William Franke. *Heythrop Journal* 51, no. 1 (2010): 174–75.

Miles, Margaret. *Augustine and the Fundamentalist's Daughter*. Eugene, OR: Cascade, 2011.

———. *Desire and Delight: A New Reading of Augustine's Confessions*. Eugene, OR: Wipf & Stock, 1991.

———. *Rereading Historical Theology: Before, During, and after Augustine*. Eugene, OR: Cascade, 2008.

Miller, Julie B. "To Remember Self, to Remember God: Augustine on Sexuality, Relationality, and the Trinity." In *Feminist Interpretations of Augustine*, edited by Judith Chelius Stark, 243–79. University Park, PA: Pennsylvania University Press, 2007.

Mojab, Shahrzad. "Muslim Women and Western Feminists: The Debate on Particulars and Universals." *Monthly Review* 50, no. 7 (1988): 19–30.

Molnar, Paul D. *Divine Freedom and the Doctrine of the Immanent Trinity: In Dialogue with Karl Barth and Contemporary Theology*. Edinburgh: T & T Clark, 2002.

Moltmann-Wendel, Elizabeth, and Jürgen Moltmann. *Humanity in God*. Cleveland: Pilgrim, 1983.

Morris, Colin. *The Discovery of the Individual: 1050–1200*. Canada: Medieval Academy of America, 1987.

Murphy, Francesca Aran. *God Is Not a Story: Realism Revisited*. Oxford: Oxford University Press, 2007.

Nadar, Sarojini. "On Being the Pentecostal Church." *Ecumenical Review* 56, no. 3 (2004): 354–67.

Nelson, Derek R. *What's Wrong with Sin*. New York: T & T Clark, 2009.

Noonan, John T. *Contraception: A History of Its Treatment by the Catholic Theologians and Canonists*. Cambridge, MA: Harvard University Press, 1966.

O'Donnell, James J. *Augsutine: A New Biography*. New York: Harper Perennial 2006.

———. "Augustine's Unconfessions." In *Augustine and Postmodernism: Confessions and Circumfession*, edited by John D. Caputo and Michael J. Scanlon, 212–21. Bloomington: Indiana University Press, 2005.

Oduyoye, Mercy Amba. *Introducing African Women's Theology*. Sheffield: Sheffield Academic, 2001.

Olson, Roger E., and Christopher A. Hall. *The Trinity*. Guides to Theology, edited by Sally Bruyneel, et al. Grand Rapids: Eerdmans, 2002.

On, Bat-Ami Bar. "Marginality and Epistemic Privilege." In *Feminist Epistemologies*, edited by Linda Alcoff and Elizabeth Potter, 83–100. New York: Routledge, 1993.

Ormerod, Neil. *The Trinity: Retrieving the Western Tradition*. Milwaukee: Marquette University Press, 2005.

Pagels, Elaine. "The Politics of Paradise: Augustine's Exegesis of Genesis 1–3 versus That of John Chrysostom." *Harvard Theological Review* 78 (1985): 67–100.

Parsons, Susan F. "The Dilemma of Difference: A Feminist Theological Exploration." *Feminist Theology: The Journal of the Britain & Ireland School of Feminist Theology* 14, no. 5 (1997): 51–72.

———. "Feminist Theology as Dogmatic Theology." In *The Cambridge Companion to Feminist Theology*, edited by Susan Frank Parsons, 114–32. Cambridge: Cambridge University Press, 2002.

Pears, Angie. "The Problematization of Feminisms and Feminist Informed Theologies in the Twenty-First Century." *Political Theology* 7, no. 2 (2006): 221–35.

Peters, Ted. *God as Trinity: Relationality and Temporality in the Divine Life.* Louisville: Westminster John Knox, 1993.

Pinnock, Clark H. "Systematic Theology." In *The Openness of God: A Biblical Challenge to the Traditional Understanding of God*, edited by Clark H. Pinnock, et al., 101–25. Downers Grove, IL: InterVarsity, 1994.

Plaskow, Judith. "Dealing with Difference Without and Within." *Journal of Feminist Studies of Religion* 19, no. 3 (Spring 2003): 91–95.

Pui-Lan, Kwok. "Feminist Theology as Intercultural Discourse." In *The Cambridge Companion to Feminist Theology*, edited by Susan Frank Parsons, 23–39. Cambridge: Cambridge University Press, 2002.

———. *Introducing Asian Feminist Theology* Sheffield: Sheffield Academic, 2000.

Rabelo, Miriam C. M., Sueli Ribeiro Mota, and Cláudio Roberto Almeida. "Cultivating the Senses and Giving In to the Sacred: Notes on Body and Experience among Pentecostal Women in Salvador, Brazil." *Journal of Contemporary Religion* 24, no. 1 (2009): 1–18.

Rahner, Karl. *The Trinity.* New York: Herder and Herder, 1970.

Reed, Esther D. Review of *Sexing the Trinity: Gender, Culture and the Divine*, by Gavin D'Costa. *Reviews in Religion & Theology* 8, no. 4 (2001): 414–18.

Robinette, Brian D. "The Difference Nothing Makes: Creatio Ex Nihilo, Resurrection, and Divine Gratuity." *Theological Studies* 72 (2011): 525–57.

Rogers, Eugene F., Jr. *After the Spirit: A Constructive Pneumatology from Resources Outside the Modern West*. Radical Traditions: Theology in a

Postcritical Key, edited by Stanley M. Hauerwas and Peter Ochs. London: SCM, 2006.

Rubenstein, Mary-Jane. "Unknow Thyself: Apophaticism, Deconstruction, and Theology after Ontotheology." *Modern Theology* 19, no. 3 (July 2003): 387–417.

Ruether, Rosemary Radford. "Augustine: Sexuality, Gender, and Women." In *Feminist Interpretations of Augustine*, edited by Judith Chelius Stark, 47–67. University Park, PA: Pennsylvania University Press, 2007.

———. "The Emergence of Christian Feminist Theology." In *The Cambridge Companion to Feminist Theology*, edited by Susan Frank Parsons, 3–22. Cambridge: Cambridge University Press, 2002.

———. "Religion, Reproduction and Violence against Women: Essays on Religion and Violence." In *Weep Not for Your Children*, edited by Lisa Isherwood and Rosemary Radford Ruether. London: Equinox, 2008.

———. Review of *Deconstruction, Feminist Theology, and the Problem of Difference: Subverting the Race/Gender Divide*, by Ellen T. Armour. *Theological Studies* 62, no. 1 (2001): 192–93.

———. *Sexism and God-Talk: Toward a Feminist Theology*. London: SCM, 1983.

Russell, Letty M. *Human Liberation in a Feminist Perspective: A Theology*. Philadelphia: Westminster, 1974.

Saiving, Valerie. "The Human Situation: A Feminine View." *Journal of Religion* 40 (April 1960): 100–12.

Sanders, John. *The God Who Risks: A Theology of Divine Providence*. Revised ed. Downers Grove, IL: InterVaristy, 2007.

Sands, Kathleen M. *Escape from Paradise: Evil and Tragedy in Feminist Theology*. Minneapolis: Fortress Press, 1994.

Schlee, Eileen. "The Subject Is Dead, Long Live the Female Subject." *Feminist Issues* 13, no. 2 (Fall 1993): 69–90.

Schmemann, Alexander. *For the Life of the World: Sacraments and Orthodoxy.* 2nd ed. Crestwood, NY: St. Vladimir's Seminary Press, 1973.

Schneider, Laurel C. Review of *Face of the Deep: A Theology of Becoming*, by Catherine Keller. *The Journal of Religion* 8, no. 4 (October 2004): 639–40.

Schüssler Fiorenza, Elizabeth. "Reaffirming Feminist/Womanist Biblical Scholarship." *Encounter* 67, no. 4 (2006): 361–73.

Shakespeare, Stephen. *Derrida and Theology.* London: T & T Clark International, 2009.

Shortt, Rupert. *God's Advocates: Christian Thinkers in Conversation.* London: Darton, Longman & Todd, 2005.

Sjørup, Lene. "Pentecostals: The Power of the Powerless." *Dialog: A Journal of Theology* 41, no. 1 (2002): 16.

Slee, Nicola M. *Faith and Feminism: An Introduction to Christian Feminist Theology.* London: Darton, Longman & Todd, 2003.

———. "The Holy Spirit and Spirituality." In *The Cambridge Companion to Feminist Theology*, edited by Susan Frank Parsons, 170–89. Cambridge: Cambridge University Press, 2002.

Smith, James K. A. "Tongues as a Resistant Discourse: A Philosophical Perspective." In *Speaking in Tongues: Multi-Disciplinary Perspectives*, edited by Mark Cartledge, 81–110. Carlise, UK: Paternoster, 2002.

Soskice, Janet Martin. *The Kindness of God: Metaphor, Gender, and Religious Language.* Oxford: Oxford University Press, 2007.

———. *Metaphor and Religious Language.* Oxford: Clarendon, 1985.

Soskice, Janet Martin, and Diana Lipton. *Feminism and Theology.* Oxford Readings in Feminism. Oxford: Oxford University Press, 2003.

Stark, Judith Chelius. "Introduction." In *Feminist Interpretations of Augustine*, edited by Judith Chelius Stark, 1–45. University Park, PA: Pennsylvania State University Press, 2007.

Strawson, Galen. "The Self." In *Personal Identity* edited by Raymond Martin and John Barresi, 335–76. Oxford: Blackwell, 2003.

Sullivan, Clayton. *Rescuing Sex from the Christians.* New York: Continuum, 2006.

Tanner, Kathryn. *God and Creation in Christian Theology: Tyranny or Empowerment?* Minneapolis: Fortress Press, 2005.

———. *Jesus, Humanity and the Trinity: A Brief Systematic Theology.* Minneapolis: Fortress Press, 2001.

———. "Trinity." In *The Blackwell Companion to Political Theology*, edited by William T. Cavanaugh and Peter Scott. Oxford: Blackwell, 2003.

Taylor, Dianna, and Karen Vintges. "Introduction: Engaging the Present." In *Feminism and the Final Foucault*, edited by Dianna Taylor and Karen Vintges. Urbana, IL: University of Illinois Press, 2004.

Thandeka. "The Self between Feminist Theory and Theology." In *Horizons in Feminist Theology: Identity, Tradition, and Norms*, edited by Rebecca S. Chopp and Sheila Greeve Delaney, 79–98. Minneapolis: Fortress Press, 1997.

Thistlethwaite, Susan. *Sex, Race and God: Christian Feminism in Black and White.* New York: Crossroad, 1989.

Toole, David. *Waiting for Godot in Sarajevo: Theological Reflections on Nihilism, Tragedy, and Apocalypse.* Boulder, CO: Westview, 1988.

Treier, Daniel J., and David Lauber. *Trinitarian Theology for the Church.* Downers Grove, IL: InterVarsity, 2009.

Turner, Denys. *Julian of Norwich, Theologian.* London: Yale University Press, 2011.

Vanhoozer, Kevin J. *Remythologizing Theology: Divine Action, Passion, and Authorship.* Cambridge Studies in Christian Doctrine, edited by Daniel W. Hardy. Cambridge: Cambridge University Press, 2010.

———. "Theological Reflections on the Claim That God Speaks (Part 1)." In *Trinitarian Theology for the Church*, edited by Daniel J. Treier and David Lauber, 25–49. Downers Grove, IL: InterVarsity, 2009.

———. "Theological Reflections on the Claim That God Speaks (Part 2)." In *Trinitarian Theology for the Church*, edited by Daniel J. Treier and David Lauber, 50–78. Downers Grove, IL: InterVarsity, 2009.

Volf, Miroslav. *Exclusion and Embrace: A Theological Exploration of Identity, Otherness, and Reconciliation.* Nashville: Abingdon, 1996.

Walker, Alice. *In Search of Our Mothers' Gardens: Womanist Prose.* New York: Harcourt Brace Jovanovich, 1983.

Ward, Graham. "Bodies: The Displaced Body of Jesus." In *Radical Orthodoxy: A New Theology,*, edited by John Milbank, Catherine Pickstock, and Graham Ward, 163–81. New York: Routledge, 1998.

———. "Deconstructive Theology." In *The Cambridge Companion to Postmodern Theology*, edited by Kevin J. Vanhoozer, 76–91. Cambridge: Cambridge University Press, 2003.

Watson, Natalie K. "Receiving Like a Woman." In *Presiding Like a Woman*, edited by Nicola Slee and Stephen Burns, 140–46. London: SPCK, 2010.

Webster, Alison. "Translating Difference: Lesbian Theological Reflections." *Feminist Theology: The Journal of the Britain & Ireland School of Feminist Theology* 21 (1999): 39.

Webster, John. "The Human Person." In *Cambridge Companion to Postmodern Theology*, edited by Kevin J. Vanhoozer, 219–34. Cambridge: Cambridge University Press, 2003.

Weedon, Chris. *Feminist Practice and Poststructuralist Theory.* 2nd ed. Oxford: Blackwell, 1997.

Weinandy, Thomas. *The Father's Spirit of Sonship: Reconceiving the Trinity.* Edinburgh: T & T Clark, 1995.

Welch, Sharon. "'Lush Life': Foucault's Analytics of Power and Jazz." In *The Blackwell Companion to Postmodern Theology*, edited by Graham Ward, 79–103. Oxford: Blackwell, 2003.

Wiley, Thata. *Original Sin: Origins, Developments, and Contemporary Meanings.* Mahwah, NJ: Paulist, 2002.

Williams, Delores. "The Color of Feminism, or: Speaking the Black Woman's Tongue." In *Feminist Theological Ethics: A Reader*, edited by Lois K. Daly. Louisville: Westminster John Knox, 1994.

———. "Sisters in the Wilderness: The Challenge of Womanist God-Talk." Maryknoll, NY: Orbis, 1993.

Williams, Rowan. "The Deflections of Desire: Negative Theology in Trinitarian Disclosure." In *Silence and the Word: Negative Theology and Incarnation*, edited by Oliver Davies and Denys Turner, 115–35. Cambridge: Cambridge University Press, 2002.

———. "On Being Creatures." In *On Christian Theology*, 63–78. Oxford: Blackwell, 2000.

———. *On Christian Theology*. Oxford: Blackwell, 2000.

———. "Prologue." In *On Christian Theology*, xii–xvi. Oxford: Blackwell, 2000.

———. "Sapientia and the Trinity: Reflections on De Trinitate." In *Collectanea Augustiniana: Mélanges T. J. Van Bavel*, edited by Bernard Bruning, et al., 317–32. Leuven: Leuven University Press, 1990.

———. "Theological Integrity." In *On Christian Theology*, 3–15. Blackwell, 2000.

———. "What Does Love Know? St Thomas on the Trinity." *New Blackfriars* 82, no. 964 (June 2001): 260–72.

Women Only Press Collective. *Love Your Enemy? The Debate between Heterosexual Feminism and Political Lesbianism*. Onlywomen, 1981.

Wolterstorff, Nicholas. *Divine Discourse: Philosophical Reflections on the Claim That God Speaks*. Cambridge: Cambridge University Press, 1995.

Zizioulas, John D. "The Doctrine of the Holy Trinity: The Significance of the Cappadocian Contribution." In *Trinitarian Theology Today: Essays on Divine Being and Act*, edited by Christoph Schwöbel, 44–60. Edinburgh: T & T Clark, 1995.

Index

CPSIA information can be obtained at www.ICGtesting.com
Printed in the USA
LVOW04s0952130115

422480LV00006BB/8/P